Presented to

_____

By

_____

On the Occasion of

_____

Date

_____

D0017110

SOUL DEEP

Prayers & Promises

ANGELA KIESLING

BARBOUR
PUBLISHING

Published by Barbour Publishing, Inc., P.O. Box 719, Uhrichsville,
Ohio 44683 www.barbourbooks.com

*Our mission is to publish and distribute inspirational products offering
exceptional value and biblical encouragement to the masses.*

ecpa Member of the
Evangelical Christian
Publishers Association

Printed in the United States of America.
5 4 3 2 1

SOUL DEEP

Prayers &
Promises

CONTENTS

PREFACE

Sometimes, prayer is easy. We're in a spiritual groove, things are going well with our friends and family, and life is good. But at other times, prayer is harder to come by. We might face relationship issues, money stresses, or physical problems that make us too tired to pray. It's all part of the up-and-down life of teenaged girls.

Soul Deep—Prayers & Promises is designed to help you through whatever your life may bring. Bible verses, speaking to specific issues of interest to teen girls, are paired with contemporary prayers, creating a book of encouragement, reflection, and challenge.

Your life is probably very busy, with school, church, family, and friends all making demands of you. But those busy periods are when prayer is most needed—and the short selections in this book will help you start a personal prayer time. If you have a specific concern, look it up in the contents pages, where topics are listed alphabetically. Feel free to expand upon the prayers and tailor them to your own personal needs. Or simply take a quiet moment to reflect on the prayer and promise as they're presented.

Spend time with God through His Word and prayer, and you'll find your spirit is strengthened at its very core—soul deep.

FITTING IN

Accept one another,
then, just as Christ accepted you,
in order to bring praise to God.

ROMANS 15:7

This is a tender subject for me, God, because I always want to fit in no matter where I go. The problem is that I shouldn't want to fit in with certain crowds. I need to strike a balance!

Maybe it's just the teenage drama, but it seems that other people's acceptance—or rejection—of me counts so much. I need Your help to tip the scale back to a balanced perspective. Deep down, I really want to be accepted by the people I respect, Lord, but I know Your opinion of me is the most important of all.

BEFRIENDING THE MISFITS

Live in harmony with one another.
Do not be proud, but be willing to
associate with people of low position.
Do not be conceited.

ROMANS 12:16

There's a crowd of kids at school that everyone else shuns, Lord. Anyone who hangs out with them is automatically labeled a geek, too. Yet when I read the Gospels, I see that Jesus hung out with the people society rejected—the misfits, the criminals, the weirdos. He didn't worry about what other people thought of Him; He just befriended anyone in need of a friend.

Every girl wants to fit in at school and be considered cool, but as a Christian I know I have to walk what I talk, which means accepting people as they are, instead of for their social status.

Even if it means drawing stares from the cool crowd, I will reach out and befriend the uncool kids, Lord. Most likely, I'll discover some wonderful friends among them.

BEYOND THE CROWD

*"You save the humble,
but your eyes are on the haughty
to bring them low."*

2 SAMUEL 22:28

Lord, You know that teenagers always say they want to be different, but when I look around the halls of my school I see several distinct groups—and the members of each look eerily alike. Some dress all in black and pierce every available part of their bodies. Others look like jocks or cheerleaders. Then there are the geeks and nerds, the cool crowd, and the misfits.

Somehow we all find our niche and stick to it like clan members. As a Christian, however, I know You have called me to reach outside my little clique and accept those different from myself.

Help me to reach beyond the "herd" mentality and make friends with anyone You bring across my path, Lord. I'm discovering it's our very "differentness" that makes us special.

A NEW TOWN

The LORD your God. . .
went ahead of you on your journey,
in fire by night and in a cloud by day,
to search out places for you to camp
and to show you the way you should go.

DEUTERONOMY 1:32–33

Moving to a new city has turned my whole world upside down, Lord! Just when I thought I'd finally found a group of kids I fit in with—and the best friend a girl could ever have—my parents announced that we were moving to another state. Help!

I know that my closest friends will always be my friends, but the miles really do form a barrier, Lord. Yes, we can talk on the phone or e-mail each other, but I'll miss the face-to-face interaction. On top of that, I'm battling loneliness and trying to fit in at my new school and new church.

Today I pray not just for acceptance in this strange new place, but for the courage to start over again.

MIRROR, MIRROR

*"But blessed are your eyes because they see,
and your ears because they hear."*

MATTHEW 13:16

It's no secret that teenage girls spend a lot of time in front of the mirror. It is both our best friend and our worst enemy. But Lord, I don't want to be enslaved by a lifeless piece of glass!

Whenever I start to obsess about my looks—whether for good or bad—direct my attention back toward You, Father. Help me to keep in mind the qualities that make a girl beautiful—an inner glow, a peace that comes from within, a vibrant smile, and eyes that shine the light of Jesus.

MAKING ME BEAUTIFUL

"Make a tree good and its fruit will be good,
or make a tree bad and its fruit will be bad,
for a tree is recognized by its fruit."

MATTHEW 12:33

The cosmetic industry must spend zillions of dollars every year convincing girls they need just one more product to make them beautiful. And Lord, You know we fall for it, hook, line, and sinker.

When I was younger, I thought wearing a little makeup would make me seem older (and of course prettier). So I started experimenting, and now I'm hooked. The funny thing is, often I hear guys say they like natural beauty more than a face full of goop.

Lord, don't let me get caught at either extreme—relying on boys for my sense of self-worth or glopping on makeup till I'm no longer "me." Your Word tells me that true beauty springs from a heart that bears good fruit. Help me to be a fruit bearer everywhere I go.

BEAUTY FOR ASHES

Bestow on them a crown of beauty
instead of ashes,
the oil of gladness instead of mourning,
and a garment of praise
instead of a spirit of despair.

ISAIAH 61:3

Lord, when I came across this verse the other day, it stopped me in my tracks. Not just its poetic grace but the overwhelming truth that You turn sorrow into joy and create something beautiful out of nothing, a pile of ashes.

My life isn't a pile of ashes, of course, but sometimes I feel like I'm struggling back from the ruins of the girl I used to be. I see my carefree nature being replaced by adult-strength worries and stress over everything from boys to my body image. Those are the times when I will turn back to this verse and claim Your promise, Lord.

Bring beauty out of the teenage havoc I've created in my life.

HOMESPUN BEAUTY

Instead, [your beauty] *should be that of
your inner self, the unfading beauty of a
gentle and quiet spirit, which is of great
worth in God's sight. For this is the way
the holy women of the past who put their hope
in God used to make themselves beautiful.*

1 PETER 3:4–5

Not everyone has the money to buy excessive beauty products and pricey, fashionable clothes. Does this mean the girl on a budget or one who wears homemade clothes can't be beautiful? Not at all! In fact, I'm discovering that a simple beauty that doesn't need products to make it shine is the best kind of all. Couple it with a heart on fire for You, Lord, and a girl has a winning combination in a world of artificial (and sometimes shallow) beauty.

Beauty is all about what's inside, first and foremost, but every girl wants to be pretty on the outside, too. Inspire me to use simple, creative touches that add sparkle to what You've placed on the inside of me.

LOVE LETTERS

Flee the evil desires of youth,
and pursue righteousness, faith, love and peace,
along with those who call on the Lord
out of a pure heart.

2 TIMOTHY 2:22

Help, Lord! I'm in love with a boy for the first time, and it's like taking a nosedive off the deep end of the pool. Every day I wake up wondering, *Will he love me back? Do I measure up to his past girlfriends? Am I even lovable?*

There's no crash course for being in love, but I've noticed You do have a few things to say about guy-girl relationships, Lord. Things like "don't awaken love before it's time" and "flee from youthful lusts." You don't mince words! I want to keep a cool head and a clean heart, Father, so help me not to lose myself over this new guy.

LOVE OR INFATUATION?

My lover is mine and I am his.

SONG OF SONGS 2:16

Every time I fall for a new guy, some adult calls it puppy love. I'll admit that at first I resented this, Lord, but now I'm starting to ask myself the hard questions: *How do I distinguish between love and infatuation? Is a crush worth losing my head (not to mention my morals) over?*

This world sends mixed messages to teens, Lord. My challenge is to filter everything I hear through Your Word. Suddenly "What would Jesus do?" is more than just a fad bracelet or a bumper sticker. It's an in-the-moment choice I have to make whenever I find myself attracted to yet another guy.

I know true love will find me when the time is right, and I'm trusting You for that perfect time—and that perfect guy.

FIRST-DATE JITTERS

Many waters cannot quench love;
rivers cannot wash it away.
If one were to give all the wealth of his house
for love, it would be utterly scorned.

SONG OF SONGS 8:7

There's nothing quite so exciting as a first date—nor anything quite so nerve-wracking beforehand. As I wait for the big night, Lord, You hear the questions zooming through my head: *Will he like me? Does this outfit make me look fat? Should I talk a lot or play it coy and quiet? Will he ask me out again?*

Ah, life with a crush! Being in love—or at least "hopeful" about a guy—is a wonderful feeling. I wake up and the sky looks bluer, my mood is lighter, I can't wait to go to school (or wherever he will be)!

At the same time I'm a bundle of nerves, always hoping I do and say and wear the right thing. I need Your peace, Father! Thanks for the opportunity to find someone special, and help me to keep this relationship honorable and pure.

BEST FOOT FORWARD

And this is my prayer:
that your love may abound more and more
in knowledge and depth of insight.

PHILIPPIANS 1:9

Lord, You know that when I'm in the first flush of love, I put my best foot forward. I'm eager for that special guy to see me look my best, act my best, be my best. But I know in a real relationship, the masks will come off and he'll see me for who I really am, "warts" and all.

At that point, true love—or a lack of it— kicks in. When a person can see me as I really am and still love me, that's unconditional love, Lord. It's the kind of love You command believers to bestow, but we often fall so short. The same is true in reverse: When I get to know a guy well enough for him to let down his guard, what kind of person do I become? Do I accept him as he is?

Regardless of the outcome of the relationship, Lord, help me to be one who loves even when the masks come off. Life is so much more than always putting your best foot—or face—forward.

LITTLE THINGS

*Praise be to the God and
Father of our Lord Jesus Christ,
who has blessed us in the heavenly realms
with every spiritual blessing in Christ.*

EPHESIANS 1:3

Lord, did I stop and thank You for all the little blessings in my life today? It's easy to focus on the big things and overlook the little things that add up to a blessing-filled life. Let me list some right now:

I'm thankful for clean laundry, hot water, flowers that border our sidewalk, and unexpected e-mails from special people. I'm thankful for ice cream, my parents, my favorite pair of jeans, and my flat iron for "frizzy" hair days.

Most of all, God, I'm thankful that I have You in my life. Thanks for being there.

WISH LIST

Surely you have granted him
eternal blessings and made him glad
with the joy of your presence.

PSALM 21:6

I think for too long I've treated You like a Santa Claus in the sky, Lord. I come to You with a notepad full of requests and a wish list that stretches for days. Please forgive me. Any real relationship goes both ways—giving and receiving—and lately I've just been on the receiving end of this one.

Somebody told me the best way to cure a greedy heart is to be thankful for what you have. So I'm declaring right now that I'm thankful for all my blessings, Lord, big and small. You are more gracious than I deserve!

BEING A BLESSING

Blessings crown the head of the righteous,
but violence overwhelms
the mouth of the wicked.

PROVERBS 10:6

Lord, I think the biggest blessings from You are not things but people. Sure, everyone loves the material blessings, but when stacked up against unforgettable moments spent with friends and loved ones, the "stuff" pales in comparison.

My prayers for blessing usually take a familiar route: *God bless all the people who are dear to me, and provide for all our needs.* But today, I want to try a different kind of prayer: *Lord, help me to be a blessing to those around me. Bring people across my path that I can help or encourage in some way. Let my life be a blessing to others as they see Your light shining through me.*

OVERFLOWING!

You anoint my head with oil; my cup overflows.
Surely goodness and love will follow me
all the days of my life, and I will dwell in
the house of the LORD forever.

PSALM 23:5–6

Father, I feel like David when he declared that his cup "overflows." You pour out so many blessings on my life, I can hardly contain them all! As I woke today, I lay in bed and thought about all the wonderful things in my life, both big and small. The big blessings—the really obvious ones—are hard to miss, but it's easy to overlook little things that are there day by day. If they were suddenly gone from my life, however, I know I would miss them.

Why do people accuse You of being a harsh God, an exacting Lawgiver with nothing but punishment on Your mind? I'm still young, but I have found You to be wonderfully personal, loving, and giving.

Thank You for the good gifts You shower on me!

CROSSING THE LINE

*Whether you turn to the right or to the left,
your ears will hear a voice behind you, saying,
"This is the way; walk in it."*

ISAIAH 30:21

Choices and consequences. I think that could be the subtitle for my entire life so far. Every time I make a choice, I'm forced to live with the results. Even though consequences aren't always fun, Lord, I've figured out why You allow them in my life—I learn from my mistakes! Each new day brings another opportunity to choose right or wrong; because You value free will, the choice is up to me.

Lord, keep my feet on the straight path today, and help me to discern the proper boundaries for my life. I want to have a life that is both exciting and safe!

TOO CLOSE FOR COMFORT

Treat younger men as brothers,
older women as mothers,
and younger women as sisters,
with absolute purity.

1 TIMOTHY 5:1–2

Lord, the more time I spend around guys—
even Christian ones—the more I realize that
keeping physical boundaries is largely up to
girls. Boys are always pushing for more physical contact, whether that means holding
hands, hugging, or beyond.

Some guys push boundaries even when
I'm not in a relationship with them. We may
be standing in line with a group of friends at
a movie theater, and suddenly he leans in way
too close to whisper something in my ear.
What should I do when somebody invades
the boundaries of my personal space?

Lord, I need Your wisdom when it comes
to dealing with boys on this issue. Help me to
gently repel the unwanted overtures and get
the message across that it's not okay to cross
boundaries unless invited to do so.

MOVIE MALADY

"Everything is permissible for me"—
but not everything is beneficial.
"Everything is permissible for me"—
but I will not be mastered by anything.

1 CORINTHIANS 6:12

Lord, I love to watch movies, but I've noticed a pattern: The more movies I see, the more I want to see, and what used to scare me seems tame now. Over time I've "advanced" from PGs to PG-13s, and now I'm tempted by kids at school who are raving about the latest R-rated films. Where will it end?

Being a Christian calls for boundaries, and movies are just one area where I feel the need to be different. Even though some people may scoff at me for my values, I'd rather keep to Your standards than gradually turn into someone I don't recognize, Lord. Give me the courage to say no when those around me are trying to influence me against my wishes.

INNOCENT GAMES?

But among you there must not be
even a hint of sexual immorality,
or of any kind of impurity, or of greed,
because these are improper for God's holy people.

EPHESIANS 5:3

Among teenagers, games like Spin the Bottle and Truth or Dare can quickly become not so innocent, Lord. I'm probably not the only Christian girl who has found herself in an uncomfortable situation more than once. At those times, you either just go along, with the approval of the crowd, or refuse to take part, branding yourself as a prude or a geek.

No one wants to feel like an outsider, but at the same time, situations do arise that call for boundaries. When those moments come— as they inevitably will—how will I choose? Will I side with the crowd or draw the line at improper behavior?

Father, give me the courage and strength to take a stand in the presence of my peers, today and every day.

PART OF A TEAM

Now you are the body of Christ,
and each one of you is a part of it.

1 CORINTHIANS 12:27

I've been learning about what the word *church* really means, Lord, and it seems we've got it all wrong. It's not a building we go to just to talk about You. It's not something we just *do*. Church is something we *are*—as believers in Jesus.

When I stop and think about what it really means to "be the church," I get excited about being a Christian. Thanks for calling me to be part of this wonderful team You've created on earth, Lord—Your church.

CHURCH CLIQUES

But when you give a banquet, invite the poor,
the crippled, the lame, the blind,
and you will be blessed.
Although they cannot repay you, you will be
repaid at the resurrection of the righteous.

LUKE 14:13–14

Lord, it goes against everything You want church to be about, but there's an "in-crowd" clique at my youth group. The girls on the inside are the prettiest, slimmest, coolest girls at church, and they know it. The problem comes when someone new tries to join in and be part of their group.

I know what it's like to be excluded, Father, and I don't ever want to be cliquish. Help me not to judge these girls, who are my sisters in Christ. Instead, inspire me to find ways to include newcomers at youth group so they feel accepted rather than rejected.

At the same time, Lord, I pray that You dissolve this harmful clique and cultivate a true body of believers among the youth at my church.

BLACK SHEEP IN THE FOLD

I praise you because I am
fearfully and wonderfully made;
your works are wonderful,
I know that full well.

PSALM 139:14

I always hear people joke about black sheep in the family, and it occurred to me it's the same way with the members of Your family, God. Only now, I think they could be describing me!

I've always been a little "different," Lord—the girl who walked to the beat of a different drummer, the one who heard another song playing—but I like being me, even if that means being different. *Especially* if that means being different!

Lord, thank You for making me unique. Help me to find my place in Your vast family and reach out to other black sheep in the fold.

BODY PARTS

*The body is a unit, though it is made up of
many parts; and though all its parts are many,
they form one body. So it is with Christ.*

1 CORINTHIANS 12:12

Your Word likens the church to a body, with
Jesus as the Head and every believer as a
functioning part of that body. This one is a
foot, and that one is a knee, and over here is
someone whose role is to be a listening ear. I
often wonder, *What part do I play, Lord? What
is my purpose in the body of Christ? Am I fulfill-
ing that role the way You want me to?*

Paul said that none of us can brag about
being more useful than anyone else because all
the members of the body are necessary. It's a
peculiar image, but maybe if I start viewing my
Christian friends this way, I'll see them in a
different light—the way You see them. No one
is a throwaway in Your kingdom, Father. We
all have a part to play and a destiny to fulfill.
Thank You for making us individually distinct
yet connected to each other through Jesus.

CURFEWS

*For in my inner being I delight in God's law;
but I see another law at work in the
members of my body, waging war against the
law of my mind and making me a prisoner of
the law of sin at work within my members. . . .
Who will rescue me from this body of death?
Thanks be to God—
through Jesus Christ our Lord!*

ROMANS 7:22–25

It seems like human nature to want to stretch the limits, Lord. If my parents say ten o'clock, I want to stay out till 10:30. If they insist on group outings, I try to bargain for a "real" date.

I don't think I'm alone in this. In his letter to the Romans, Paul described the same thing. He said he did what he didn't want to do and didn't do what he wanted to do—and he wrote half of the New Testament!

I know my parents only want what's best for me, Lord. Every time I feel that fighter instinct rise to the surface, knock it back down for my own good. Someday I may be a parent, too!

STAYING TRUE TO MYSELF

It is because of him that you are in Christ Jesus,
who has become for us wisdom from God—
that is, our righteousness,
holiness and redemption.

1 CORINTHIANS 1:30

Lord, I have to ask myself, *What effect does my relationship with a boy have on my personality? Do I become disorganized, unfocused, dreamy, destructive, or can I honestly see that this person brings out my best?*

I've decided on a new plumb line: If I'm not myself when I hang out with a guy, then we shouldn't be together. At the same time, he should let me be myself—and not force me into being or doing something I'm not.

Father, help me to "keep my head" when I'm crazy over some boy. I want to be true to myself and to You.

TOO SOON?

For this reason,
since the day we heard about you,
we have not stopped praying for you and
asking God to fill you with the knowledge
of his will through all spiritual wisdom
and understanding.

COLOSSIANS 1:9

How do I know when it's the right time to date—or whether I should date at all? I know that one school of thought says to "kiss dating good-bye," while others approve of dating with careful guidelines. What do You think about the whole subject, Lord?

I flip-flop between wanting to go out with boys and preferring to wait for "courtship" with that one special guy You've created for me. If I look to the trend of culture, the choice is easy—date as many boys as possible and the cuter the better.

I know Your way is perfect, Lord, and that You provide wisdom through my parents and Your Word. Make the choices clear as they come up every day of my life.

GROUP DATES

*May the God who gives endurance
and encouragement give you a spirit of unity
among yourselves as you follow Christ Jesus.*

ROMANS 15:5

Parents are always in favor of group dates, and I guess it's no wonder. We girls are a lot more likely to remain "safe"—literally and figuratively—when more than one person (a boy) is around! From what I can tell, You don't even lay out a guide for "smart dating" in the Bible, Lord. All I can find is the verse about how it is "good for a man not to touch a woman." And the best way I know of to avoid physical contact is not to be alone in the first place.

Some of my best memories are of times hanging out with friends from youth group, whether a barbeque or a car wash or a whole gang of us going to the movies together. These group outings give me the chance to meet boys and talk to them one-on-one, but still within the safety of the "herd."

Thanks for the many opportunities to be with people my age in a fun, wholesome environment, Father!

THE BOY BAROMETER

Do not be yoked together with unbelievers.
For what do righteousness and
wickedness have in common?
Or what fellowship can
light have with darkness?

2 CORINTHIANS 6:14

At times I get so confused when it comes to dealing with guys at school or youth group. This crazy attraction for the opposite sex was Your idea, Lord, but I need Your help in figuring out how to navigate the waters!

My biggest struggle comes from measuring my worth by what boys think of me. *Am I pretty? Am I cool? Am I fun to be around?* Yet deep down inside I know that the right boy will like me for who I am—whether that means I'm "cool" or not. A guy who puts You first will also have my best interests at heart.

Steer me clear of relationships that could cause pain, Lord. I want Your best for my life, even if it means waiting a long time for someone special to come along.

BEST OF BOTH WORLDS

Finally, all of you,
live in harmony with one another;
be sympathetic, love as brothers,
be compassionate and humble.

1 PETER 3:8

Sometimes I think just having a guy "friend" is better than having a boyfriend. Do You know why, Lord? Boyfriends bring out the heavy emotions in us girls, and sometimes we lose all sense of perspective on everything else in life. Our homework may suffer, our family relationships may take a backseat, our jobs or household chores may get less than our best—all because we're obsessed with a boy.

In contrast, a good guy pal can be not only a best friend but also a window into the weird world of boys—from a safe distance! Without all the emotional baggage that goes with a relationship, we can be ourselves around a true guy friend and learn how to interact with the opposite sex.

In my heart, Lord, I believe this is the better way. Help me to cultivate platonic friendships with one or two worthy guys—guys that put You first in their lives.

GO FIGURE!

There are three things that are
too amazing for me,
four that I do not understand:
the way of an eagle in the sky,
the way of a snake on a rock,
the way of a ship on the high seas,
and the way of a man with a maiden.

PROVERBS 30:18–19

They say females are hard to figure out. I'm feeling the very same way about boys, Father. What were You thinking when You made this crazy half of the species?!

No matter how much I try to get inside the mind of the opposite sex, I blunder and fail miserably. Maybe that's part of the mystique between male and female. Maybe that's why I care so much, even when I don't want to!

Help me to keep my head when dealing with boys, Lord. I don't want to get in too deep at this point in my life. Still, I've gotta say: Boys rule!

KEEPING MY IDENTITY

*I pray that out of his glorious riches
he may strengthen you with power
through his Spirit in your inner being.*

EPHESIANS 3:16

Ah, now here's a topic I could talk about for days. In fact, sometimes I do! Boys—what to do about them, Lord? They're confusing yet wonderful. My biggest struggle is not to lose my sense of self when I'm caught up in a swoon over some boy. At school, everyone classifies the girls into "has boyfriend" and "no boy-friend" categories. What does that say about the girls *without* a boyfriend? Are they deficient, lacking in some pertinent way?

Lord, help me to keep my own identity and not get lost in what boys think of me—if they even think of me at all. Someday I'll be able to look back on these teen years and laugh, but right now I'm in the thick of battle, and it's mainly a battle of self-esteem.

LIGHT IN THE TUNNEL

Look on me and answer,
O LORD my God.
Give light to my eyes,
or I will sleep in death.

PSALM 13:3

Even though I'm normally upbeat, I can get depressed over anything from my body image to not being accepted by the in-crowd at youth group. Depression stinks! They call it a Prozac Nation, but I've found that the best antidote to the blues is talking to You, Lord, or reading certain Scriptures that relate to what I'm going through.

When my heart feels heavy or circumstances seem beyond my control, remind me of Your infinite promises in the Bible. It's amazing to think that a book so old can be so relevant to a girl in the twenty-first century!

THE SLOUGH OF DESPOND

I waited patiently for the LORD;
he turned to me and heard my cry.
He lifted me out of the slimy pit,
out of the mud and mire;
he set my feet on a rock and
gave me a firm place to stand.

PSALM 40:1–2

Lord, I've read *The Pilgrim's Progress*, and in it, the character Christian encounters many obstacles on his way to the celestial city. One of them is a swamp called Despond—in modern terms, I'd call that depression.

Why is it that faith and doubt go hand-in-hand? Why do my struggles to live right sometimes land me in the Slough of Despond, Lord? When I first said yes to You, I thought the Christian life would be easy, but I've discovered that things don't always work out the way I want them to.

I'm starting to realize that doesn't mean failure, though; it just means I grow through my struggles. Like Christian, help me through the dark swampy places in life, Father.

IN THE SCARY PLACE

When men are brought low and you say,
'Lift them up!'
then he will save the downcast.

JOB 22:29

I've heard of a girl who missed three weeks of school due to a vague "illness" before her parents realized she was acutely depressed. Sadly, depression seems to be epidemic among my peers, Lord—especially the girls. We live in a time that puts adult pressures and adult temptations on teenagers before they can even drive a car.

When I feel my own spirits sink to a frightening low, remind me of Your nearness, Lord. Give me the energy to turn to You through prayer or reading Scripture. Prompt a friend or family member to call me with an encouraging word.

Depression can be a scary place, Father. Help all those who can't find the strength to hang on anymore. Help them to hang on to You.

MY HEAD OR HORMONES?

*I have great sorrow and
unceasing anguish in my heart.*

ROMANS 9:2

Sometimes I can't tell what's causing me to feel so low—PMS or the circumstances of my life. When I get depressed, Lord, it's like viewing the world through dark glasses, and that darkness colors my entire reality. As soon as the depression lifts, life returns to normal.

I know girls are more prone to moodiness because of monthly hormone fluctuations, but that shouldn't always get the blame for my bleak perspective. Life is simply sad sometimes, Father, and at those times I feel the weight of the world on my shoulders, even at my age.

I need a mood lifter today, Lord. Help me to make it through the day!

BATTLE OF THE BULGE

*A happy heart makes the face cheerful,
but heartache crushes the spirit.*

PROVERBS 15:13

Yuck! I looked in the mirror today and saw a new bulge. So here I am worrying about how to lose that extra weight. Was life really meant to be a constant battle with the scale?

In today's world, body image is everything, but once again I come up against the knowledge that I'm living in a parallel universe, so to speak—a world ruled by a different set of values and a different master. Lord, be the voice that I hear speaking whenever I get depressed about my weight. Remind me that I am more than what the scale and that unforgiving full-length mirror say I am. Beauty is so much more than skin deep!

DANGEROUSLY THIN

So God created man in his own image,
in the image of God he created him;
male and female he created them.

GENESIS 1:27

Lord, so many girls I know practically starve themselves to be thin. Before long, their whole world revolves around what to eat, what not to eat, how much (or little) to eat, and what they look like in their favorite pair of jeans. When their collarbones look bony and they still complain of being fat, I know they've hit the danger zone.

I worry about my body image, too, Lord. Sometimes that means I yo-yo diet when I know better, but so far I've been able to draw a line between dieting and starving myself.

Help me to keep a balance with food and exercise so that I maintain a healthy weight but never compromise safety for a lithe look.

MINUTE CHOICES

*This day I call heaven and earth as witnesses
against you that I have set before you life and
death, blessings and curses. Now choose life,
so that you and your children may live.*

DEUTERONOMY 30:19

Like any challenge, dieting—or rather healthy eating—boils down to a minute-by-minute choice. If I feel a familiar rumble in my stomach, I face a choice: cookies or an apple? A doughnut or raisins?

Lord, the culture we live in doesn't do much to help, but I know that ultimately the choice is mine whether to indulge in something healthy right now or not. When I view smart dieting in this manner, suddenly it's not such an overwhelming task. Instead of planning a week's menus or even a day's, I only have to worry about the next bite that goes into my mouth.

I know that food temptations will come, Lord, and I want to be strong enough to overcome them. Help me when my willpower grows weak.

WILLPOWER

*"Will you rely on him for his great strength?
Will you leave your heavy work to him?"*

JOB 39:11

Like anything worth doing well, dieting takes serious willpower. Or should I say, *healthy eating* takes willpower (the "D word" is a no-no these days). But, like anything requiring willpower, dieting is not easy to do. It's easy to start dieting but very difficult to stick with it. That's what I'm appealing to You about, Lord.

You made my body to be a certain size and shape, and I'm generally comfortable with that. What I'm not comfortable with are the extra pounds that have crept onto my thighs and waist.

While strength of will may not be considered a spiritual thing, I need Your help anyway, Lord. Give me the true grit to "just say no" to wrong foods.

LIFE BOUNDARIES

For these commands are a lamp,
this teaching is a light,
and the corrections of discipline
are the way to life.

PROVERBS 6:23

My difficulty with discipline is in knowing my boundaries and not overstepping them, whether it's eating right or not caving in to peer pressure. I see guidelines in Your Word about discipline—people who faced impossible situations and still maintained their boundaries. I want that kind of inner strength, too, Lord.

Whenever I feel weak or ready to compromise in some area, remind me that discipline is definitely worth the effort in the end.

NEAT FREAK

The proverbs of Solomon son of David,
king of Israel:
for acquiring a disciplined and prudent life,
doing what is right and just and fair. . .

PROVERBS 1:1, 3

Some people struggle with sloppiness, while others go overboard being a neat freak. You know where I fall on that scale, Lord, and just how much I strive to find a balance.

I know life is more than where I put my socks or learning not to obsess over crooked wall hangings. Still, this trait seems ingrained in me—and it drives me crazy when I'm around polar opposites.

Help me to discipline my life, Lord, not just to balance my extremes but to have patience with those not like me. We're all as variegated as flowers in a flowerbed.

MILE MARKER

*May he give you the desire of your heart
and make all your plans succeed.*

PSALM 20:4

It helps me stick to a plan when I have guide-posts and mile markers by which to track my progress. Suppose I want to commit to spending one hour a night studying for a final. If I make a checkmark on my calendar after each successful attempt, the days tick off quickly and the goal seems closer in sight. I know the same is true for any goal in my life.

In a way, this is a lot like how You work with me, Lord. You provide people and events that serve as guideposts through life, so I won't lose my focus on the goal. When I have these outward "mile markers," I am encouraged to keep going and not lose heart.

Thank You for keeping me disciplined!

LOVING CORRECTION

Because the LORD disciplines those he loves,
as a father the son he delights in.

PROVERBS 3:12

Your Word says that You discipline those You love, just as a father corrects a wayward son. At face value, that doesn't sound like the kind of Scripture I want to post on my bathroom mirror! But when I think about it or dig a little deeper, I realize that promise is bathed in love.

They say that young children who grow up with no discipline—no boundaries to keep them safe—feel insecure and live in constant fear of abandonment. Kids always roll their eyes when a parent says, "This is gonna hurt me more than it hurts you," but deep down we know that a parent who disciplines us really must love us. It's the uncaring parent who doesn't bother with correction.

The next time I feel Your gentle correction in my life, Lord, help me to respond immediately so that I don't have to learn the lesson twice!

OPPOSITES ATTRACT

Be merciful to those who doubt.

JUDE 22

People say that opposites attract, so maybe that's why faith goes hand in hand with doubting. No matter how hard I try, Lord, a period of spiritual highs is always followed by lows—those times when I doubt myself, doubt my parents, doubt my faith, even doubt You.

When I was younger, I imagined life as a Christian would be easy—just follow the Golden Rule and love God with all your heart. The rest would take care of itself, I figured. Now I'm realizing that anything worth living for must also be worth dying for and that hard questions and soul-searching go hand in hand with deeper levels of faith.

Walk with me today, Lord, and hold me up when doubts come my way.

NIGHTTIME DOUBTS

On my bed I remember you;
I think of you through the watches of the night.

PSALM 63:6

Why is it that problems seem bigger at night and worries put in overtime in the dark? I think I'm starting to see a pattern here, Lord. My doubts about You grow disproportionately large when I turn out the lights. Those nighttime doubts may have caused me to toss and turn in the past, but I'm ready for a change.

Tonight as my head touches the pillow, I will remember Your promises and fall asleep with the name of Jesus on my lips. Nothing can stand in the way of Your Word in my life.

NEVER TOO LATE

The fruit of the righteous is a tree of life,
and he who wins souls is wise.

PROVERBS 11:30

Lord, I'm praying diligently for that person who needs to know You in a personal way. I've read stories about people who prayed for someone for thirty years before they became believers, and I'm wondering, *Can I hang in there that long? Will I have the prayer patience and stamina to keep pleading on this person's behalf?*

Whenever I start to doubt the likelihood that this person will get saved, remind me again of Your infinite patience and grace. Until our last breath, it's never too late to say yes to Jesus.

DOUBTING MY ABILITIES

The LORD preserves the faithful,
but the proud he pays back in full.

PSALM 31:23

For some people, arrogance is a problem. I suffer from the exact opposite issue: not believing in myself and my abilities enough. When I consider myself objectively, I know You have gifted me to do certain things well and other things very well. The things I can't do well don't need to drag me down; instead, if I see them as Your special gifts to other people it helps me keep it in perspective. We can't all be good at everything!

Lord, whenever I'm tempted to downgrade my abilities or when I lack the courage to try something new, remind me that through You I am more than a conqueror! Don't let me wallow in self-pity or remorse if I do pass up an opportunity. Rather, help me to get back on my feet and try again.

DREAM-MAKER

"And afterward,
I will pour out my Spirit on all people.
Your sons and daughters will prophesy,
your old men will dream dreams,
your young men will see visions."

JOEL 2:28

When I hear the word *dream,* two things come to mind: the stories that run through my head at night and the visions of great things I want to do someday. It's this last kind that means so much to me, Lord.

Sometimes I lie awake at night and think about what my life will be like—the things I long for and aspire to be. Will they come true, Father? Will I be able to look back on my life as an old woman and know that it was a life lived well? Plant Your dreams in my heart, and plot out my days so that those dreams come true!

REVISED PLANS

*But the noble man makes noble plans,
and by noble deeds he stands.*

ISAIAH 32:8

I used to dream of big things I wanted to do, Lord. Then something unexpected happened: I outgrew those dreams and discovered new ones germinating in my heart!

It seems to me the dreaming process never ends, and I never want it to. What I used to think of as getting off track I now see as revised plans or rejuvenated goals—especially when they seem to come straight from Your heart to mine.

Let me never stop being a dreamer, Lord, but keep me centered on Your perfect will for my life. Together we can accomplish great things!

ENCOURAGING OTHERS' DREAMS

Therefore encourage each other with these words.

1 THESSALONIANS 4:18

How easily I become self-centered when the subject of dreams comes up, Lord. Immediately my mind focuses on the goals and visions I hope to accomplish in life, with little thought to how I can help others with their dreams.

What a revolutionary idea: I can help others fulfill their dreams by encouraging them when their spirits sag, brainstorming ideas to accomplish their dreams, and participating with them in activities that will help them reach their goals.

Dreams can seem unattainable when we stand years away from their fulfillment, but when a helpful friend dreams with us, it makes the "getting there" more manageable—and definitely more fun!

BEST FOR LAST

*"Everyone brings out the choice wine first
and then the cheaper wine after the guests
have had too much to drink;
but you have saved the best till now."*

JOHN 2:10

Sometimes, when I hear the stories of older people's lives, I begin to see a pattern in the way You work in human lives, Lord. Often it seems You save the best for last. Seen from the greedy perspective of youth, this might seem unfair, but in Your wisdom I think You make us wait for the best things so that we season over time.

It gives me hope when I hear people talk about cherished dreams that finally came true —sometimes years after the dream was birthed. Like Abraham, we grow through the testing of our faith and the patience that is worked into our character over time.

Lord, You know how impatient teenagers are, yet still You offer grace for the taking. Make me a wise and patient dreamer. I know that in my life, as in the wedding at Cana, You will save the best wine for last.

TURNING FROM EVIL

"Produce fruit in keeping with repentance."

MATTHEW 3:8

Every day brings a new set of choices my way, and the free will You've given me allows me to live for or against Your values, Lord.

I've heard that the word *repent* really means "to change one's mind"—to go in a different direction or to turn away from something. Repentance isn't a very popular word in today's world, but it describes the heart change I want to make every time I realize I've made a bad choice. Not just a stupid mistake, Father, but a decisive choice to go against what I know is right.

Help me to turn from evil today, and don't let me be attracted to things that are harmful to me. I want to love what You love and hate what You hate—sin.

MORE THAN JUST A TREND

*Your word is a lamp to my feet
and a light for my path.*

PSALM 119:105

I'm learning that evil is not how you look; it's how you act. It's more than just dressing in black and listening to creepy music. Our culture is consumed with evil, Lord, and I realize now how subtle it can be. By degrees I feel the pull of its influence, but I want to live a life that stands out against it—a life that shines the light of Christ.

Help me to resist evil, Lord, no matter what face it wears. Today I will choose the path of righteousness and shun everything that smacks of evil. Allow me the chance to show my peers that there's a different path they can choose.

A WRONG FASCINATION

Avoid every kind of evil.

1 THESSALONIANS 5:22

Lord, I see that our world feeds an undercurrent of fascination with evil and the supernatural that strikes me as very dangerous. I don't have to look very hard to find it: books, TV shows, video games, movies, and the Internet all portray evil as glamorous—a fascinating journey into personal power.

As a Christian teen, I'm all too aware of how much this flies in the face of Your Word, Father. You tell me to shun evil and to avoid things that have even the appearance of evil. As I strive to stand up for righteousness in this dark world, shine Your light through me—especially into the lives of people I love who are flirting with evil right now.

FALSE RELIGIONS

The acts of the sinful nature are obvious:
sexual immorality, impurity and debauchery;
idolatry and witchcraft; hatred,
discord, jealousy, fits of rage. . .

GALATIANS 5:19–20

There's a pervasive attitude today that any road to God is a good road. Many say we simply take different paths, but they all lead to You. According to Your Word, Lord, this is an outright lie! In fact, the apostle Paul called these false religions and Christian half-truths "doctrines of demons." Pretty strong language, but I know he said it for a reason.

For example, I've heard that Wicca is the fastest-growing religion on college campuses and that it's enormously popular with teenage girls, too. I don't have to look too far to see "goddess" messages and mystical emblems even at my school.

Father, help me to take a stand for righteousness whenever the time comes to speak up—and let me know when it's time to speak up. I don't want to see my generation snared by a newly packaged form of the same old witchcraft You tell us to avoid in Your Word.

What Now?

Blessed is the man who listens to me [wisdom],
watching daily at my doors,
waiting at my doorway.

PROVERBS 8:34

The question looming in my mind today is,
Lord, what now? I blew it big-time and feel
pretty lousy about it. The good news for me is
that I'm in great company. As I flip through
the pages of my Bible, I read story after story
about other people who messed up, got off
track, even rebelled for a while and still went
on to do great things for You. I guess my story
isn't finished yet either.

Please help me to get back on my feet
today, and keep writing the pages of my life—
the way You want them to be. I need Your
wisdom every day!

BLOWING IT

But God, who comforts the downcast,
comforted us.

2 CORINTHIANS 7:6

Whenever I blow it big-time, Lord, my self-esteem plummets through the floor and I don't even care to crawl back up. At that overwhelming moment, all I can see is the missed opportunity and what I should have done differently.

Beating myself up mentally is something I do well, Lord, and it's a behavior I want to change. I suppose we all struggle with failure; letting ourselves—or, worse, others—down is the worst feeling in the world. But in reality, I know there are worse things in the world.

The psalmist turned to You whenever he was discouraged about something. He also wrote his thoughts down or turned them into songs. Maybe I'll try journaling my thoughts in a written prayer to You, Lord. Like the psalmist, I know You have others plans for me. This one disappointment is not the end.

ENCOURAGING OTHERS

I do not hide your righteousness in my heart;
I speak of your faithfulness and salvation.
I do not conceal your love
and your truth from the great assembly.

PSALM 40:10

Sometimes the hardest failure to take is that of a close friend or family member. When the hopes of someone we love are on the line, we feel the pain of failure intensely. In doing so, we actually fulfill one of Your gentle commands, Lord—to mourn with those who mourn. In time, we'll be able to rejoice with them as well.

Never let me be flippant in the face of another's failure. Instead, I want to give an encouraging word, a "You can do it!" from the heart.

I'm learning that failure is as much a part of life as celebration. Both are needed to mold us into people who rely on You, Lord.

NOT THE END

Therefore I do not run like a man running aimlessly; I do not fight like a man beating the air. No, I beat my body and make it my slave so that after I have preached to others, I myself will not be disqualified for the prize.

1 CORINTHIANS 9:26–27

Lord, I've learned in history that Abraham Lincoln failed numerous times before getting elected President of the United States. And people scoffed at inventors like Benjamin Franklin and the Wright brothers—until they saw electricity harnessed and a strange new vehicle take flight.

Failure in life can be devastating, especially for a teenager. Insecurity is practically stamped on our foreheads. Yet I'm starting to realize that failure doesn't have to be an end. Like Lincoln, we can use our failures and mistakes as springboards to a new effort. They say with every attempt you increase your likelihood of achieving success.

Whenever I face failure in life, Lord, help me to get back on my feet and realize the race is still going on.

Blind Faith?

*Now faith is being sure of what we hope for
and certain of what we do not see.*

HEBREWS 11:1

Father, Your Word says, "Faith is the substance of things hoped for, the evidence of things not seen." What an awesome thought! It sounds like an oxymoron, but that's what makes faith so cool.

Whenever someone accuses me of having "blind faith," I'll point them toward these mind-blowing words in Scripture and tell them what I've discovered in my own life: Just because something doesn't make sense to the rational mind doesn't mean it can't be true.

Thanks for opening my eyes to the "evidence of things not seen."

THE ONLY WAY IS UP

Where can I go from your Spirit?
Where can I flee from your presence?
If I go up to the heavens, you are there;
if I make my bed in the depths,
you are there.

PSALM 139:7–8

My spirits hit rock bottom today, Lord, and I almost despaired. Then I remembered something I once heard: When you hit the bottom, the only way to go is up!

Actually, my faith in You isn't supposed to get that desperate, but if I'm honest, I know that my faith muscle needs to grow. Don't let me wait for rock bottom to exercise my faith, Lord. Stretch me and grow me until my faith biceps bulge with strength. I want a life of confident belief, not one of timidity or despair.

PILLARS

So then,
just as you received Christ Jesus as Lord,
continue to live in him,
rooted and built up in him,
strengthened in the faith as you were taught,
and overflowing with thankfulness.

COLOSSIANS 2:6–7

I've heard an old-fashioned phrase that refers to strong believers as pillars of the faith. When I think of pillars, Lord, I picture the huge Gothic kind that hold up balconies on massive buildings. A pillar is a physical and spiritual symbol of strength.

Lord, it would be incredible to grow so strong in my faith that someday people refer to me that way! Though I'm still young, already I can appreciate how the faith walk is a step-by-step, day-by-day process. Sometimes it even feels like three steps forward, two steps back. But You have promised in Your Word that You will finish the work You began in me. It's awesome to know I have a divine Craftsman building me into a pillar of faith!

SET APART

But you are a chosen people, a royal priesthood,
a holy nation, a people belonging to God,
that you may declare the praises of him who called
you out of darkness into his wonderful light.

1 PETER 2:9

My faith makes me different from others, Lord—at least different in a spiritual sense. It's almost shocking how few kids my age grew up in church or know even basic Bible stories. Being different will always make me feel a bit apart from the crowd, but that's not really a bad thing, especially when I see the direction the crowd is headed in.

In Your Word, Lord, You call believers the sons and daughters of God—"a royal priesthood, a holy nation"—people who are set apart from the rest of the world for Your holy purpose. It blows my mind to think that I am the daughter of a King, and that this King wants to have a personal relationship with me!

Whenever I start to feel odd because of my beliefs, Father, remind me that the same goes for any true believer, and that the price is well worth the reward in the end.

WHAT IS FAITHFUL?

Dear friend,
you are faithful in what
you are doing for the brothers,
even though they are strangers to you.

3 JOHN 5

I've been thinking of what the answer to that question, "What is faithful?" may sound like, Lord, and the best I can come up with is "Doing what is right in Your sight." Would You agree?

I want to be faithful not just in the Christian sense—reading my Bible, spending time alone with You, sharing my faith—but also in the little things of life: helping my mom around the house, doing my best on schoolwork, being there for a friend who's hurting.

Lord, *faithful* is a word I'd like to be known for every day of my life, so keep me mindful that my choices have consequences!

BEING DEPENDABLE

*Each one should use whatever gift
he has received to serve others,
faithfully administering God's grace
in its various forms.*

1 PETER 4:10

Lord, I want to know that I can always depend on others, but I also have to wonder, *Can others depend on me? Can my parents, siblings, friends, teachers, and church leaders count on me when it really matters?*

"Dependable" may sound like a description of a Labrador, but it's something I want to be, Father. I'd like to be the friend someone calls in the middle of the night if crisis strikes. I want to be available to my family in good times and bad. I hope to be remembered as a person who went out of her way to be reliable.

No matter what we call it, dependability is the character trait that will draw others in times of real need. Mold me into that type of person, Lord.

FOLLOWING THROUGH

It gave me great joy to have some brothers
come and tell about your faithfulness
to the truth and how you
continue to walk in the truth.

3 JOHN 3

If I say I'm going to do something, I need to deliver—and that is so much more difficult than just saying the words. Lord, I'm realizing how often people (including myself) toss off promises and commitments with our mouths then fall short of following through. But everything I read in Your Word demonstrates that faithfulness—even in the little things—matters more than what we say in the first place.

Lord, give me the wisdom to think through what I say before I say it and to avoid promising things I may not be able to deliver. Even if others chalk it up to "just the way things are," I know You expect better of me. In short, character counts.

MORE THAN EXPECTED

Love and faithfulness meet together;
righteousness and peace kiss each other.

PSALM 85:10

Being faithful as a daughter, as a sister, as a friend, as a believer, demands a lot! Yet I find that the load is light because it's a privilege to be a Christian teen. So many of my peers are troubled and caught up in the world's darkness. Being a light bearer for You in the midst of a searching world gives meaning and purpose to my life.

Lord, help me not just to be faithful but to go beyond the call of duty—to do more than is expected of me. Since others are watching my actions as a believer, I want to do and be my best.

SIBLINGS

Be devoted to one another in brotherly love.

ROMANS 12:10

Lord, sometimes being a sister feels like the hardest thing I do. When my siblings drive me crazy, I need an extra bit of grace to get through the day!

It's funny, but I just realized they may feel the same way about me, too sometimes. When You walked the earth, Jesus, You always showed compassion and forgiveness to everyone You met. Help me to see my brothers and sisters through Your eyes and love them—even when the feeling isn't there.

When I'm honest with myself, I have to admit that being a sister is a pretty cool thing. Thank You for my siblings, Lord. Who else is going to sand off my rough edges the way they do?!

EXTENDED LOVE

God sets the lonely in families.

PSALM 68:6

Lord, when I think about families, it seems that modern times, easy mobility, and the fast pace of life have all pushed them farther and farther apart geographically—and maybe even relationally. I hear stories about how families used to grow up and live in a single town their entire lives. Social gatherings included members of the extended family, with aunts, uncles, cousins, and grandparents all a part of a child's life. That kind of extended family love must create a strong anchor in a young person's life, but so many kids my age are missing all the components of even a nuclear family—no wonder we seem fragmented!

Lord, I know that You promise to be a Father to the fatherless and that You "set the lonely in families." Thank You for all the members of my family, both near and far. May I never take them—or their love—for granted.

GETTING ALONG

*Make every effort to keep the unity
of the Spirit through the bond of peace.*

EPHESIANS 4:3

It's been said that families are Your way of teaching us how to get along with others, Lord. When I stop and think about it, that's probably true. In a family, you don't get to pick who your brothers and sisters are. You don't get to choose your parents. They just come as they are—a package deal, like it or not. People even joke about how every family has its weirdos and misfits, its clowns and control freaks.

The challenge, then, is to get along with these diverse people and love them in spite of all their quirks. They sure have to deal with mine! The good news: As I learn to love sometimes unlovable people, I'm getting free training in how to interact in the world at large.

My family is a little wacky at times, Lord, but I wouldn't trade them for the world!

KEEPING THE CLAN TOGETHER

*Therefore, as we have opportunity,
let us do good to all people, especially to those
who belong to the family of believers.*

GALATIANS 6:10

In this day and age of transient love and short-term marriages, kids can start to feel lost in the shuffle, God. You placed us in families for our nurture and protection, but even those qualities sometimes get battered by the cruel realities of the world we live in. When I start to feel like I'm sinking, remind me that You are the real Head of my family—and the One who holds it together.

I look around me and see other kids who are in really frightening circumstances—maybe Mom left with a new boyfriend or Dad went out for cigarettes one night and never came home. When I hear these stories, I am thankful all over again for my own little clan and what each individual member of my family means to me.

We're not perfect, Lord, but we are a family.

THINGS THAT GO
BUMP IN THE NIGHT

*You will not fear the terror of night,
nor the arrow that flies by day.*

PSALM 91:5

The world can be a scary place, Lord. Even my room freaks me out some nights, when the furniture creaks or I hear strange sounds through my bedroom window. Maybe a movie I watched put fearful thoughts in my head, or the news broadcast reported a violent crime close to my home.

You promise in Your Word to keep me safe and to give me "sweet sleep" at night, Father. Whenever I have a white-knuckle night, I realize all over again what a blessing restful sleep is. Help me not to be afraid but to trust in You when I see shadows that shouldn't be there or when my mind is filled with fear. I want to take hold of Your promise every night of my life!

NO FEAR!

"Peace I leave with you;
my peace I give you.
I do not give to you as the world gives.
Do not let your hearts be troubled
and do not be afraid."

JOHN 14:27

A line of clothing called *No Fear!* used to be popular. Every time I saw the logo I wondered, *What are we supposed to have no fear of? Does it apply to life in general?*

I think the only true way to experience "No Fear" is to hook into You, God. There's no guarantee that I won't be afraid in this life, but You tell me I don't have to be afraid. It's all about trusting You—something that feels like the challenge of the century on certain days.

Today, let "No Fear" be my motto—not because of some shirt logo but because You are an awesome God!

FEAR OF ABANDONMENT

*For you did not receive a spirit that makes you
a slave again to fear, but you received the Spirit
of sonship. And by him we cry, "Abba, Father."*

ROMANS 8:15

The biggest fear factor for most kids growing
up is not the death-defying feats they show on
reality TV shows. Rather, I think it's the fear of
abandonment. Regardless of my home situation, the fear that someone I love will abandon
me is always just at the back of my mind.

Where does this innate insecurity come
from, Lord? You certainly have never aban-
doned me, and You promise never to do so.
But it's the humans in my life that I can't be
so sure of. Maybe, as babies and toddlers, we
worried that when Mom or Dad went away,
they would never come back. Maybe something like that really happened later in our
lives. Perhaps a trusted friend betrayed us, or
a boyfriend cast us aside for someone else.

Whatever form the abandonment takes, it
hurts, Father—deeply. When I'm seized with
fearful thoughts of abandonment, hold my
hand fast and remind me that You will always
be there.

Danger Zone

*Even though I walk
through the valley of the shadow of death,
I will fear no evil, for you are with me;
your rod and your staff, they comfort me.*

Psalm 23:4

As much as we try to avoid scary situations—people and places that can bring nothing but harm to us—every girl finds herself in the danger zone now and then. Maybe it's a dark, lonely street when our car battery gives out or a party we thought would be innocent but turns out to be far from it. Whatever the situation, we can't always see danger coming, and when we find ourselves in way over our heads, it's time to cry out to You, Lord.

The Bible says You have not given us a spirit of fear, but a spirit of power, love, and a sound mind. Whenever I find myself in frightening circumstances, remind me that You will be with me in the dark valleys of life. Though danger lurks all around me, I know that You have sent angels to guard me and guide me back to safety.

Forgiving Myself

*Create in me a pure heart, O God,
and renew a steadfast spirit within me.*

PSALM 51:10

Forgiving others is a difficult thing to do, but I'm discovering that forgiving myself can be hardest of all. For some reason I am my own worst critic, and when I fall short of my expectations—not to mention Your expectations, Lord—I struggle to forgive myself.

I know You always accept me just as I am and forgive me when I slip up. Teach me how to extend that same grace to myself, Jesus. I want to shine Your light in my life.

YO-YO GRACE

"If your brother sins against you,
go and show him his fault,
just between the two of you.
If he listens to you,
you have won your brother over."

MATTHEW 18:15

I forgave someone the other day, and now I want to take it back. Isn't that just like human nature, Lord! How exasperated You must be when You look down from heaven and see the way I act.

I know that true forgiveness is a once-for-all deal. There's no such thing as yo-yo grace, here one minute and snatched away the next. Yet sometimes I treat other people that way.

When I look in Your Word, Lord, I see a different standard altogether. You forgave people on the spot, then told them to "go and sin no more." No condemnation, no guilt trips—just grace. Help me to have that kind of grace for others.

FORGIVE US OUR DEBTS?

*"Forgive us our debts,
as we also have forgiven our debtors."*

MATTHEW 6:12

Lord, there's a line in Your prayer that really used to confuse me: "Forgive us our debts, as we forgive our debtors." I would recite the words along with everyone else in church and think, *Huh? What debts do I owe that need forgiveness from You?*

Now I understand it's not talking about money or a "pound of flesh." Rather, my debts are the sins I commit against You, either consciously or unconsciously. You are calling me to forgive others the wrongs they commit against me, just as You forgive me the wrongs I commit against You.

What a freeing thought! Seen in that light, forgiving others is no longer a wearying task or heavy load. It becomes my privilege to extend grace to others because You gave Your grace to me first. What an awesome God You are!

SEVENTY SEVEN TIMES

*Then Peter came to Jesus and asked,
"Lord, how many times shall I forgive
my brother when he sins against me?
Up to seven times?" Jesus answered,
"I tell you, not seven times,
but seventy-seven times."*

MATTHEW 18:21–22

Jesus, there's a parable You told that used to puzzle me. It's the one about the ungrateful servant who wouldn't forgive a small debt owed to him after he was forgiven a very large debt by his master.

When Peter asked You how many times he should forgive his brother, he thought he was being very righteous when he guessed "seven." But Your answer shocked him, "Not seven times, but seventy-seven times."

But who's keeping count? I think that's the whole point of this passage—instead of keeping a checklist of wrongs, I am called to forgive others endlessly, as You forgive me, Lord.

Best Friend Blues

To the faithful you show yourself faithful,
to the blameless you show yourself blameless.

PSALM 18:25

What happens when my best friend lets me down or, worse, doesn't want me for a friend anymore? I never expected to be heartbroken over a girl! What am I doing wrong, Lord?

When I was younger I took friendships for granted, but now I'm starting to see that true friendship—like any real relationship—takes work and commitment. Father, help me to see where I've fallen short in this friendship, and give me the wisdom to love unconditionally. I want to be the best friend I can be.

MAKING ROOM FOR MORE

"But when you give a banquet,
invite the poor, the crippled,
the lame, the blind."

LUKE 14:13

I've known what it's like to be a best friend—someone else's favorite person in the whole world—but then get squeezed out by a new friend who steals my best friend's time and attention. Jealousy flares up within me, Lord, and I feel slighted, rejected for someone "better."

Who would have thought girl friendships could sometimes be as tricky as guy/girl relationships? Just when I thought I'd found a friend who would be there for me through thick and thin, I got ousted.

Lord, help me to be a gracious friend to everyone and not play favorites. Now that I know what's like to be hurt by a friend, I don't want to inflict that pain on another. Let me view all people as the gift they are.

BETTER THAN A SISTER

*"Greater love has no one than this,
that he lay down his life for his friends."*

JOHN 15:13

Thank You for my best friend, Lord. She is wonderful! I remember how long I prayed for a special friend and how astonished I was when I realized she wanted to be my friend. She really, truly, genuinely wants to be with. . .me!

When I was younger, friends and play-mates came easily, but now I've reached the age where I choose friends more carefully. And whom I choose makes all the difference.

As we grow older together, wrap our friendship in Your grace, Lord, and remind us daily of what a gift we have in each other. There's nothing like having someone you can be yourself around.

SHYNESS

*Be kind and compassionate to one another,
forgiving each other,
just as in Christ God forgave you.*

EPHESIANS 4:32

A lot of people seem to outgrow shyness as they get older, but I'm stuck here in the phase where it can attack the most! I guess a certain amount of insecurity goes along with being a teenager, but I don't need the extra pressure of being shy, Lord.

To make matters worse, some kids mistake shyness for snobbiness. I've been accused of being stuck-up, but when people got to know me, they couldn't believe how different I was from their first impression. In reality, I'm about as down-to-earth as possible, and I want to put everyone at ease in my company. Help me to get over the jitters when I'm meeting someone new, and give me the confidence to introduce myself first.

I know that to have friends you have to be a friend, so I want to overcome my shyness and reach out to new people who may be longing for a friend, too.

WARPED PLANS

*Delight yourself in the LORD
and he will give you the desires of your heart.
Commit your way to the LORD;
trust in him and he will do this.*

PSALM 37:4–5

Lord, something didn't work out the way I wanted it to—the way I thought it would—and I'm frustrated. I feel as though everything I've worked so hard for just blew up in my face.

When my plans go awry, I know it's time to put my focus back on You and allow You to open the right doors for me. Maybe I got ahead of You this time; maybe this just wasn't Your best for my life. Keep me on track with Your will, Lord—that's really where I want to be.

MY WAY OR THE HIGHWAY?

*. . .so that the body of Christ may be
built up until we all reach unity in
the faith and in the knowledge of
the Son of God and become mature,
attaining to the whole measure
of the fullness of Christ.*

EPHESIANS 4:12–13

Growing up is all about learning to compromise, I'm discovering. Not compromising in
the bad sense of the word, but learning to give
and take—instead of demanding my way like
a spoiled toddler.

Sure, I still get frustrated, Lord, and I
imagine that's just an ongoing part of life. But
now I'm starting to see things through a different lens. These days when I get frustrated,
instead of freaking out or pouting, I want to
turn the situation over to You. After all, You
said in Your Word to cast all my cares on You
because You care for me.

FAMILY FEUDS

I appeal to you, brothers, in the name of our
Lord Jesus Christ, that all of you agree
with one another so that there may be no
divisions among you and that you may be
perfectly united in mind and thought.

1 CORINTHIANS 1:10

My family is driving me crazy, Lord—especially that one particular person who will
remain unnamed! No matter how much I try
to bite my tongue when I'm around, an argu-
ment erupts and I get pulled into the fight.
Then we battle it out and give each other the
silent treatment for days.

Every family goes through this stuff, I'm
sure, but something tells me it shouldn't be
this way. We're human beings, not cats and
dogs. Where's the love?

Prayers for endless agreement seem unrea-
sonable, so just for today I ask You to keep my
temper in check, Lord. Make me a kinder person, and when my fuse runs short, extend it by
Your grace. For my part, I will commit to con-
centrate on the good traits in people and try to
see them through Your eyes.

OVERLOOKED

Wait for the LORD;
be strong and take heart
and wait for the LORD.

PSALM 27:14

It happened again. I was passed over in favor of someone more talented, better looking—or whatever excuse I can scrounge up in my frustration, Lord. The truth is probably not so extreme, but it hurts to be overlooked when I thought I was perfect for the opportunity.

Dealing with frustration is just one part of growing up that I didn't count on when I was younger. Back then, my parents took care of everything. If something didn't happen, I took it in stride in my innocent, childish way—not analyzing it to death like I do now.

Father, teach me how to cope when disappointment comes and frustration sets in. I guess this is part of the learning process, too.

ONE DAY AT A TIME

Do not those who plot evil go astray?
But those who plan what is good
find love and faithfulness.

PROVERBS 14:22

I saw a bumper sticker the other day that read
"One Day at a Time." I think it has to do with
a twelve-step program, but I've decided to make
it my own personal motto. Whenever I start
thinking about the future, I get anxious and
wonder, *Will I marry the right man? Will I land
a good job? Will I fulfill my destiny as a believer?
What if the world ends before I get a chance to do
all these things?*

Lord, I know You have a perfect plan for
my life. Help me to rest in the knowledge that
You will guide me every step of the way, even
far into the future.

TOMORROW

Consider the blameless,
observe the upright;
there is a future for the man of peace.

PSALM 37:37

I used to lie awake in my bed and leap light-years into the future. The result? I freaked out about way too many things. Instead of trying to plot out my whole life, I'm going to start focusing on today—and maybe even tomorrow, Lord. That's not looking too far ahead, is it?

Today is here and now, but it's quickly passing. Tomorrow is still full of promise. Help me to live in such a way that all my todays are meaningful and all my tomorrows are still golden—and full of promise.

IS THE END IN SIGHT?

Listen, I tell you a mystery: We will not all sleep, but we will all be changed—in a flash, in the twinkling of an eye, at the last trumpet. For the trumpet will sound, the dead will be raised imperishable, and we will be changed.

1 CORINTHIANS 15:51–52

People are saying the end of the world is near. All the prophetic signs are falling into place, they say—it won't be long. Whenever I hear these things or read Revelation for myself, I get mixed emotions. One part of me longs for Your return, Lord, and the other part just wants the chance to grow up, get married, and have children of my own.

Will my life here on earth be cut short? I suppose there are no guarantees, and the Bible says the life we will live with You in heaven far surpasses anything we could dream of.

The bottom line, I guess, is that my future—and the future of the whole world—is in Your hands, Father. Help me to live wisely and make the best use of the time allotted to me, whether it's ten more years or eighty.

LITTLE OLD ME?

Gray hair is a crown of splendor;
it is attained by a righteous life.

PROVERBS 16:31

Sometimes I stop and think about what it will be like to be old. In particular, I wonder what kind of old woman I will be, *Will I be the little old lady children love to be around? Or will I grow dour and cold, sending a message of "stay away" to everyone?* I've seen elderly people whose light shines like a beacon, but I've also seen the kind everyone wants to cut a path around.

As I grow older, Lord, keep my spirit young and my heart open to the working of Your grace. I want to age gracefully and graciously, showing the world that joy is available to anyone who walks with You.

SELFLESS

*For those who are self-seeking
and who reject the truth and follow evil,
there will be wrath and anger.
There will be trouble and distress
for every human being who does evil:
first for the Jew, then for the Gentile.*

ROMANS 2:8–9

Lord, the whole riptide of culture pushes me to be selfish—self-serving, self-seeking, self-promoting, self-indulgent. But I see a different current at work in the pages of Scripture. Instead of a taker, I am called to be a giver. Instead of hoarding, You ask me to give freely.

Jesus, You promised that the same "measuring stick" I use in giving to others will be used with me. No, I don't want to give to *get*, but it's wonderful to know that all my needs—and even some delightful wants—will be provided by You.

A HELPING HAND

*"In the same way,
let your light shine before men,
that they may see your good deeds
and praise your Father in heaven."*

MATTHEW 5:16

Lord, I realize that giving is so much more than the money I drop in the offering plate at church or the bag of clothing I donate to Goodwill. Giving is any kind, selfless act that springs from my heart to benefit another. With that as a working definition, I think I can give more than I ever thought possible.

I can help my little sister with her homework—no strings attached. I can offer a helping hand to elderly people in my neighborhood. I can let someone else shine instead of taking all the glory for myself. I can even go out of my way to talk to the girl no one likes at school.

When I read the accounts of Your life, Jesus, I see a giver in action. Over and over again You gave and expected nothing in return. That's the kind of person I want to be, too.

HELPING THE POOR

Jesus answered,
"If you want to be perfect,
go, sell your possessions and give to the poor,
and you will have treasure in heaven.
Then come, follow me."

MATTHEW 19:21

Instead of just a religion, You call us into a relationship with You, Father. And in describing righteous actions, You have a lot to say about taking care of the poor. It's funny how often that facet of Christianity is forgotten when it's something You stress so much in the Scriptures.

Now I have to turn the spotlight inward, *Do I do my part to care for the poor? If not, how can I start? What can I do?*

Give me wisdom and grace as I begin to reach out to others less fortunate than I am. I also pray for creative ways to bless the poor—things that include more than giving them money. I want to be a giver and inspire others to give as well, Lord. Keep me faithful in this endeavor.

UNAWARE

"But when you give to the needy, do not let your
left hand know what your right hand is doing,
so that your giving may be in secret.
Then your Father, who sees what is done
in secret, will reward you."

MATTHEW 6:3–4

Jesus, when You talked about giving, You mentioned how *not* to give—in a boastful manner that draws the attention of others. The Pharisee loudly poured clinking coins into the temple coffers—and discouraged the heart of God for his showiness. The poor woman tossed in a penny—and won the praise of heaven.

Your standard is "don't let the left hand know what the right hand is doing." In other words, when giving and doing good deeds becomes ingrained in my character, I won't even "notice" when it happens.

Today as I go about my daily activities, bring people across my life whom I can bless through the giving of my time, my attention, and possibly even my possessions. Cultivate a godly "unawareness" as I reach out to others in a helping manner!

AIMING HIGH

*Do you not know that
in a race all the runners run,
but only one gets the prize?
Run in such a way as to get the prize.*

1 CORINTHIANS 9:24

So many kids today seem to think that slacking off is cool, something to be admired, but everything I hear about high school reunions proves the opposite to be true. The cool kids often end up going nowhere while the geeks and nerds accomplish their goals and live their dreams.

I know You have great plans for my life, Father, and I want to fulfill that destiny. Since each day is like another piece of the puzzle dropped into place, help me to make the choices today that will lead me in the right direction. Plant Your dreams in my heart, and steer me toward the goal You have in mind.

Each day is so much more exciting when I realize it's another step of the journey You have planned for me!

SETBACKS

But you are a shield around me, O LORD;
you bestow glory on me and lift up my head.

PSALM 3:3

When I'm so close to a goal and miss the mark, my whole world comes crashing down. Lord, it's tempting to have a pity party, but I know even the most successful people in the world have setbacks. I'm no different.

My attitude is everything, I'm discovering. If I get down in the dumps and wallow there, my mood will pull me even lower. But if I choose to think positively and try again— whether the same goal or a new one—I find renewed energy for the task at hand.

Let me learn from Paul, who found contentment and zeal in every situation—because he knew he had a high calling.

REALISM VS. IDEALISM

*Do not conform any longer to
the pattern of this world,
but be transformed by the renewing of your mind.
Then you will be able to test
and approve what God's will is—
his good, pleasing and perfect will.*

ROMANS 12:2

I've heard it said that a cynic is just a disappointed idealist—someone who started out with high hopes and lofty goals but got worn down by disappointment and unfulfilled dreams. What a contrast I see in Your Word, Father! There, You encourage me to live and dream big, but also to rely on You for the fulfillment of those dreams. It sounds like the perfect balance between cautious realism and far-flung idealism.

How do I maintain a balance with my own goals and dreams? Never let me settle for less than Your best, Lord, but teach me to stay within Your perfect will for my life. I know if I follow the path You've laid out before me, I can't go wrong.

GETTING STRATEGIC

> *. . .for attaining wisdom and discipline;*
> *for understanding words of insight;*
> *for acquiring a disciplined and prudent life,*
> *doing what is right and just and fair.*

PROVERBS 1:2–3

They say that if I write my goals down, I'm much more likely to achieve them. Sounds like a very simple thing to do—a little effort that could potentially pay big dividends. Yet it's so easy to get lazy when it comes to setting goals. I have a goal in sight and even think about it a lot, but I don't always actively plot out my strategy for achieving it. This is one area in which I need to make changes in my life, Lord!

Lord, keep me faithful and disciplined as I plot out the steps to the really big goals in my life. But along the way, I want to stay just as committed in the small things, too.

Who Me?

*Therefore, there is now no condemnation for
those who are in Christ Jesus.*

ROMANS 8:1

Okay, I admit sometimes I feel guilty, Lord.
Why? Well, You know the reason why. Hard
as I try, I can't seem to live up to Your standards for godliness in every area of my life. As
soon as I get one area under control, another
one blows up in my face.

Something I read in Your Word the other
day shed some light on this whole guilt thing.
I found out that You don't condemn me when
I fall short of the mark; rather, You convict
(or convince) me of the need to do what's
right. Seen in that light, messing up is okay
as long as I get back on my feet and keep
moving forward.

NOT GUILTY!

"Come now, let us reason together,"
says the LORD.
"Though your sins are like scarlet,
they shall be as white as snow;
though they are red as crimson,
they shall be like wool."

ISAIAH 1:18

Those words, when handed down from a judge at a trial, are words of life and freedom. They mean, literally, that someone can go free. No penalty, no punishment necessary—not guilty!

Because of Your death on the cross, Lord, the words "not guilty" ring out across my life. I don't have to wallow in guilt about a misspent past; I don't need to rerun the shameful tapes in my head. I have been washed clean by Your loving gift on the cross.

Thank You, Jesus, for taking my penalty and letting me go free!

A CLEAN CONSCIENCE

How much more, then,
will the blood of Christ,
who through the eternal Spirit
offered himself unblemished to God,
cleanse our consciences from acts
that lead to death,
so that we may serve the living God!

HEBREWS 9:14

I think You placed within every human heart the capacity to know right from wrong, Lord. And when I do something wrong, my conscience goes off like a siren. Sometimes I try to ignore it, to push that little red flag out of my vision—but it's still there, and I know it.

Help me to keep a clean conscience before You, Father. I don't want to struggle all the time and grieve the Holy Spirit. How much better it would be to live by the parameters of the guidance You have placed within me.

Today, my prayer is that I not only listen to my conscience but that I also obey it—the very first time it sounds the alarm!

GLUTTONY

He who keeps the law is a discerning son,
but a companion of gluttons
disgraces his father.

PROVERBS 28:7

I just pigged out, eating way more than I should have, and now I'm feeling guilty, Father. Even though it's not scriptural, I can see why they call gluttony one of the seven "deadly" sins—it's deadly all right! I indulge in some food, revel in the taste sensations for a little while, stuff myself, then wallow in regret.

Help me to exercise control when I'm at the table, on the run (my biggest temptation—fast food), or eating out with family or friends. The phrase "all things in moderation" definitely applies here, but I need a little boost when temptation comes.

ANOTHER SAMUEL?

The LORD came and stood there,
calling as at the other times,
"Samuel! Samuel!"
Then Samuel said,
"Speak, for your servant is listening."

1 SAMUEL 3:10

A story I remember from Sunday school tells how, as a boy, the prophet Samuel heard You calling him in the night. Nothing so dramatic has ever happened to me, Lord, but I know I "hear" Your voice just the same.

When a Scripture verse leaps off the page and speaks right to me, that's Your voice. When a friend says just the right thing to lift my spirits, that's You speaking through her. When the lyric of a song reminds me of Your love, it's like the Holy Spirit whispering in my ear.

Thank You for all the ways You speak in my life, Lord. I don't ever want to stop hearing Your voice.

VOICES

Love the LORD your God,
listen to his voice, and hold fast to him.
For the LORD is your life,
and he will give you many years
in the land he swore to give to your fathers,
Abraham, Isaac and Jacob.

DEUTERONOMY 30:20

I've heard of people who hear voices in their head. That's downright creepy, and not at all what I mean when I tell others that You talk to me, Lord! I'm glad I have a living relationship with You, the Creator of all things! I'm not ashamed to tell others that I speak to You and—amazingly—You speak back.

Being a Christian gets a bad rap in today's world, but I've decided it's really a pretty cool thing. Whenever I want to, I can talk to the Maker of heaven and earth, who loves me, just as I am.

Lord, thank You for calling me to Your side. I don't ever want to stop walking and talking with You!

MY BEST FRIEND

The LORD would speak to Moses face to face,
as a man speaks with his friend.

EXODUS 33:11

When I stop and think about it, talking to You is really like talking to a friend, Lord—my best friend. I used to think of prayer as a monologue in which I told You everything that was troubling me and then asked You to fix it. Or, perhaps I needed a few things and was sure You would happily provide them.

Then, when my faith started to grow a little deeper, I noticed a change in the way I talk to You. Now it's more like a two-way conversation, a chat between friends. People ask me how I know You talk back, and all I can tell them is that I simply know. Not in an audible voice, of course, but Your words and intentions find their way to my heart.

Thanks for being my best friend, Jesus.

FILTERING

"Hear me, you who know what is right,
you people who have my law in your hearts."

ISAIAH 51:7

Most of the time I want to hear Your voice, Lord, and I'm thankful that You talk to me in the many ways You do. But I have a confession to make: Sometimes I intentionally block the sound of Your voice. I filter the truth that comes into my spirit because it opposes the thought or deed I am intent on doing.

Selfish? Yes. Foolish? Absolutely. I can relate to the apostle Paul when he laments about the state of his heart—wanting to do one thing but doing another.

Father, instill within me the "want to" so that I never shut out the sound of Your voice. Create in me the desire for more of You, even when what You say is not what I want to hear.

TRUTH TELLERS

Jesus answered,
"I am the way and the truth and the life.
No one comes to the Father except through me."

JOHN 14:6

It's funny, Lord—I want other people to be honest with me all the time, but sometimes I'm afraid to tell other people the truth. Maybe what I have to say will hurt them in some way, so I shy away from it. Maybe I lack the courage to tell the whole truth and nothing but the truth—so I tell a "white lie" instead.

Starting today, Lord, I want to be a truth-teller no matter what the situation. Keep me accountable, and help me to remember that You *are* Truth. When I embrace truth, I shine Your light into a false world.

WHITE LIES

"When he [the devil] *lies,*
he speaks his native language,
for he is a liar and the father of lies."

JOHN 8:44

It's expected behavior to tell "little white lies" in today's world. We think that only an idiot would incriminate herself by telling the whole truth. But lately, Lord, I've started to realize that a half-truth is still a lie.

If honesty is the code of a believer, then help me to be truthful everywhere I go, with everyone I meet, Lord. In the end, a lie is more costly than the truth anyway, because if I tell one lie, then I have to tell another to cover up the first one.

Make my tongue a reliable source, Lord; teach me when to hold it and when to speak up.

HURT BY LIES

A truthful witness does not deceive,
but a false witness pours out lies.

PROVERBS 14:5

When a friend or family member lies to me, and I find out, my trust in them instantly dies. I guess that's why they say trust is one of those character traits that has to be earned, like respect.

Is it too much to expect total honesty from those closest to me, Lord? I hope not, because I'm sure they expect the same from me (and why shouldn't they?). Yet I know we all fall short in this area sometimes, even when we "intend" to be completely honest.

Make me a truth seeker and a truth teller everywhere I go and with everyone I encounter, Lord. Lies hurt and destroy, but truth heals and restores.

TRANSPARENT

Do not be misled:
"Bad company corrupts good character."

1 CORINTHIANS 15:33

Take everything else away—all the trappings and posturing—and I will still be me, just me. The teen years are a difficult time in which to be transparent, but I've decided that's exactly what I want to be, Lord.

When everyone else is hiding behind a façade or acting the way they think they're supposed to act, prompt me to stand out by being simply and truly myself. Being transparent—letting others see the real me—is just another form of honesty, and that seems like a nonnegotiable character trait in the life of a Christian!

UNFAILING HOPE

*But the eyes of the LORD
are on those who fear him,
on those whose hope is in his unfailing love.*

PSALM 33:18

Since becoming a Christian, I've noticed how much more hopeful I am. Sure, I get depressed like everyone else, but just knowing You're there beside me keeps me from sinking too low, Lord.

No matter what happens or how bad things seem to get, I always have hope in Your unfailing love for me, Lord—love that gives me unfailing hope because I know You died and rose again to give me life with You forever.

Let me shine the light of that unfailing hope into others' lives today!

LAST BEST CHANCE

Guide me in your truth and teach me,
for you are God my Savior,
and my hope is in you all day long.

PSALM 25:5

When everyone else has given up on me, Lord, You are my last best chance—my only hope. That gives me reason to hope all by itself!

I know the days ahead in my life will hold both sorrow and happiness. Refuel my spirit with Your peace and joy today, so that I will have reason to hope for tomorrow.

Never let me lose sight of who You are, Father. If I stumble, pick me up. If my faith begins to thin, give me renewed hope.

FRESH START

*Because of the LORD's great love
we are not consumed,
for his compassions never fail.
They are new every morning;
great is your faithfulness.*

LAMENTATIONS 3:22–23

Just as every new year gets depicted as a "baby" year—fresh and young and full of potential—every new day is the same. At least that's how I'm determined to see it, Lord. When I wake up in the morning, I will know I'm starting with a clean slate. If I made mistakes the day before, I have a brand-new chance to try again. If my mood was lousy the day before, I have a new beginning. No matter what happened yesterday, today is a new day full of possibilities.

Let me live today to the fullest, Father, and pack every minute with meaning!

WHEN HOPE FALTERS

But the needy will not always be forgotten,
nor the hope of the afflicted ever perish.

PSALM 9:18

There's an unrealistic expectation that many Christians hold over the heads of other believers: namely, that we should never be depressed or lose hope. But Lord, I wonder if that's realistic? I look in the Psalms and read words of melancholy from David. He got as low as a human can go, but he also ended his songs with a declaration of hope. It's almost as if he were commanding his heart, "Be cheerful! God is still in control!"

When my hope falters, Lord, let me take a cue from David and speak words of faith in spite of the circumstances. Somehow, things always get better in the end.

Plugged In

*But godliness with contentment
is great gain.*

1 Timothy 6:6

It's not realistic to be happy all the time, but I think the quiet sense of joy You give me is a never-ending emotion. It's like being plugged into the Source.

Being a girl (and a teenager no less), I know I'll have ups and downs in life. Yet it's good to know that no matter what happens, Your Spirit is still there inside me, burning bright and steady. Today may bring happiness or sorrow, but that doesn't mean I will lose my joy, Father. Teach me to be like Paul—content in every situation and abounding in joy.

JOY BREAKS

For what is our hope, our joy,
or the crown in which we will glory in the
presence of our Lord Jesus when he comes?
Is it not you?

1 THESSALONIANS 2:19

Mini-moments of joy sprinkled throughout my day make all the difference, Lord. These little pick-me-up times can be as simple as a phone call from a friend or reading a good book at bedtime with my cat curled up beside me.

It's so easy to get caught up in the quick pace of life and forget to savor these little God-sent moments that add joy to my life. Today, I want to make an intentional effort to count my "joy breaks."

Thank You, Father, for showering me with these special times.

IT'S A WONDERFUL LIFE

You have made known to me the path of life;
you will fill me with joy in your presence.

PSALM 16:11

Yes, that's the name of an old (and somewhat cheesy) movie, but I have to agree, Father; it *is* a wonderful life, as long as You're in it. That doesn't mean every day is picture-perfect or that I always get what I want. It simply means life—this chance to live and breathe and do and experience—is wonderful because You made it to be an adventure.

Teenagers are famous for their moodiness, and I guess I'm no exception. When those downer days come around, remind me of how precious life is and what a joy it is to live every moment with You.

Unexpected Joys

"I have told you this so that my joy may be
in you and that your joy may be complete."

John 15:11

Life scatters small joys here and there and occasional big surprises that land in your lap unexpectedly. I think these are best kind, Lord.

Unexpected joys come in all shapes and sizes. They may take the form of people who visit after a long absence, a friendship that suddenly blossoms into romance, or something as dramatic as a sick loved one recovering from a deadly illness.

In all the ways You shower me with joy, I take delight, Lord. Help me to be an unexpected joy in someone's life today.

SWEET SOLITUDE

He makes me lie down in green pastures,
he leads me beside quiet waters,
he restores my soul.

PSALM 23:2–3

I've made an amazing discovery, Lord. The "cure" for loneliness is solitude—time spent alone with You. I don't always have to be with other people to feel accepted or special. When I really listen with my heart, I hear Your voice whispering, "It's okay—I'm here." You give me all the support and company I will ever need.

Being human, sometimes I do long for companionship—the flesh-and-blood kind. But even in this, Lord, I want Your input. Bring the right people across my path, and let me be a blessing to them first.

With You as my "soul mate" I can never truly be lonely. Thank You for promising never to leave me or forsake me.

TABLE FOR ONE

Why are you downcast, O my soul?
Why so disturbed within me?
Put your hope in God,
for I will yet praise him,
my Savior and my God.

PSALM 42:5–6

Right now it's just You and me, Lord. I feel like no one else wants to be with me, and that's a jagged little pill to swallow. The funny thing is, I've discovered that some of Your favorite people spent lots of time in solitary confinement. David cried out to You from caves; Joseph ended up in a prison far from home; Jesus spent His last night on earth all alone. Well, alone with You, Father.

When I get discouraged and feel like no one wants my company, remind me of how special I am in Your eyes. Let me sense Your presence in the quiet hours, Lord.

Like shadows on a painted landscape that emphasize the light, help me to see loneliness as a necessary part of life. The truth is that even when I'm loneliest of all, I'm never really alone.

INSTANT MESSENGER MIRACLE

O my Strength, I sing praise to you;
you, O God, are my fortress, my loving God.

PSALM 59:17

I was lonely tonight, Lord, so I logged onto the computer to "talk" online with my friends. When I checked my buddy list, I saw one special friend I hadn't connected with for a while. We IMed for half an hour, and when she finally signed off, I stopped to think about what her friendship means to me—and how much it helped chase away the blues to talk tonight.

I know You're always there, too, Lord, waiting for me to "log on" and chat about my day. It's good to know I don't need a "shopping list" when I approach You in prayer. Instead, let's just talk!

Liking My Own Company

*But Jesus often withdrew
to lonely places and prayed.*

Luke 5:16

I suppose everyone gets lonely from time to time and longs for companionship. The thought of spending a lot of time on my own—with no one but myself for company—used to bother me, Lord. I spent the whole time trying to think of ways I could shorten my solitude and be with other people again.

As I grow older, I'm finding that sometimes it's good just to savor the times alone—with no one but You and me, Lord. The Bible says Jesus sought lonely places where He could commune with You. What a great example to follow!

Little by little, I'm starting to like my own company, and I think that's a very good thing. Thanks for making me who I am, Father, even with all my quirks! I like who I am, and I especially like the person I am when I'm with You.

FAKE FRIENDS

A man of many companions may come to ruin,
but there is a friend who
sticks closer than a brother.

PROVERBS 18:24

I thought she was for real, but I found out my friend wasn't the person I thought she was. It hurts to realize someone is less than what you think, Lord. Now I'm wondering, *Do people ever think the same of me?*

I want to be a true friend to the people in my life, even if that means showing them the "real" me. It's scary to drop the masks and be yourself. Yet it's so much better to relate mask-free than to find out the hard way that someone is a fake friend.

Help me to be the kind of friend that "sticks closer than a brother"—or sister!

NONNEGOTIABLES

Jonathan said to David,
"Go in peace, for we have sworn friendship
with each other in the name of the LORD, saying,
'The LORD is witness between you and me,
and between your descendants
and my descendants forever.' "

1 SAMUEL 20:42

Lord, I think when it comes to friendship and family, loyalty is one of those nonnegotiable traits; we should simply be loyal because the relationship demands it. An unwritten code keeps both parties honorable. At least, that's the way it should be.

Sadly, what I see in the world around me doesn't always hit that high-water mark. People use each other and discard "friendships" if they cease being useful—that is, if their "friends" stop serving their own needs.

Lord, help me to be the kind of friend, daughter, and sister who is in a friendship for the long haul, no matter what happens.

WHOM WILL I BELIEVE?

*Now it is required that those who
have been given a trust must prove faithful.*

1 CORINTHIANS 4:2

Lord, life can sure throw curve balls sometimes. Like the times when I hear a rumor about a friend that shocks me to the core. I wonder, *Could it be true?* then try to dismiss the thought.

When faced with a choice between believing a rumor or the word of the one talked about, I will choose to give that person the benefit of the doubt. I guess it's sort of like our judicial system—innocent until proven guilty. By choosing to go against the grain, I demonstrate faith in my friend and become an example for others to follow. Maybe the rumor will turn out to be true. If so, I will extend grace to my friend as You have poured out grace on me.

STAYING TRUE

To the faithful you show yourself faithful,
to the blameless you show yourself blameless.

PSALM 18:25

Being loyal to friends and family is a lifetime calling, isn't it, Father? Everything about our culture reeks of impermanence—instant gratification, but no promise for the long haul. I guess the same mentality goes for loyalty: Sure, I'll be your friend as long as things are cool between us. Everything comes with a condition.

But when I look in Your Word, I see a radical departure from the world's point of view. Loyalty is something we give simply because You call us to be faithful in everything.

Some of my relationships have received less than my best, Lord, but starting today I want to change that. Help me to be a loyal, faithful friend.

BAGGAGE

Brothers, I do not consider myself
yet to have taken hold of it.
But one thing I do:
Forgetting what is behind
and straining toward what is ahead,
I press on toward the goal to win
the prize for which God has
called me heavenward in Christ Jesus.

PHILIPPIANS 3:13–14

The apostle Paul had some good thoughts about what to do with the past—leave it behind and press on toward the calling I have in You, Jesus.

Regrets and bad memories can really weigh a person down, but whenever I choose to leave them where they belong—in the past—my mind feels like a heavy load's been lifted.

Lord, help me not to dwell on the past but to treasure each moment that belongs to me today. I know I'll still make mistakes, but at least with You holding my hand I can get back up!

Starting Over

What benefit did you reap at that time
from the things you are now ashamed of?
Those things result in death!
But now that you have been set free from sin
and have become slaves to God,
the benefit you reap leads to holiness,
and the result is eternal life.

Romans 6:21–22

Lord, I've done some things I'm ashamed of, and now I want a fresh beginning. I hope to start over and put these bad memories behind me. Will You show me how to do this?

It's remarkable how much grace You give to someone like me. My actions could brand me as sinful, but instead they end up drawing me back to You, asking forgiveness and the chance to make a new start. The awesome reality is that You are a God of second chances! Not just for me, but for anyone who needs it.

Give me the wisdom to turn from wrong choices in the future, and help me to start down the straight and narrow path once again.

BAD MEMORIES

As far as the east is from the west,
so far has he removed
our transgressions from us.

PSALM 103:12

Your Word says You put all my sins in the sea of forgetfulness, Lord—"as far away as the east is from the west." In fact, it says You remember our sins no more.

What an incredible thought! I wish I had the ability to wipe my memory slate as clean as You do, Father. Sometimes memories of things I did in the past leap up to haunt me or get me down. I don't want to dwell in the past, though. With Your Holy Spirit living inside me, I know I am a new creation. The past doesn't matter anymore. Those old sins and bad memories are gone as far as You're concerned—help me to see them the same way.

LIFE MEMORIES

Surely goodness and love will follow me
all the days of my life,
and I will dwell in the house
of the LORD forever.

PSALM 23:6

Sometimes it feels like I'm growing up too fast, Lord, but isn't that what every teenager wants? We're always in a rush to be adults, but then I hear adults talk wistfully about their childhoods. Maybe we just always want what we don't have.

I once heard an old person say the "golden years" are always just five years behind you. That made me stop and think that if that's so, then these teen years I'm living right now will be my "golden years" just a few years down the road.

Lord, help me to treasure each moment of every day and live life to the fullest. I want *every* year to be a golden year, no matter how old I grow to be. And while I'm on the journey, let me remember to stop and say thanks for every day.

Hang in There!

Wait for the LORD and keep his way.

PSALM 37:34

Help! I need patience, Lord, and I want it now—just kidding! That's my attempt at making light of a serious subject. But seriously, what do I do when I can't stand to wait any longer for something or someone important to me?

Everything I've read in the Bible about patience tells me to wait on You. In my heart I know You have a perfect timetable for everything—it just doesn't always fit my grand scheme!

Lord, help me to wait on You instead of always leaping ahead. I'm sure it will be worth the wait!

NEVER GIVE UP

*Bear in mind that
our Lord's patience means salvation.*

2 PETER 3:15

It amazes me how patient You are with me, Lord. If I were You, I'd have given up on me—and this whole crazy world—a long time ago. Yet You gently and graciously prod me in the right direction, pick me up when I fall, steer me back on track, and whisper instructions to help me along the way. You even send just the right person at just the right time to walk along with me.

When I think about my faith walk, I get excited about what the future holds. And with You as my patient guide, I know I'll make it to the finish line. Who could ever accuse Christians of leading dull lives?

THE RIGHT ONE

Daughters of Jerusalem, I charge you:
Do not arouse or awaken love until it so desires.

SONG OF SONGS 8:4

Waiting for the guy who's right for me is like waiting for a double rainbow to appear over my house—it's possible, but I can't make it happen. Worse, the more I long for it, the more it seems to elude me. Suddenly everywhere I look I see happy couples all googly-eyed over each other. When will that happen to me, Lord? When will it be my turn?

I just reread that last line, and I realize it sounds so whiny. Even though I do want to love and be loved exclusively, I know that—like a double rainbow—the right guy for me is very rare. He's one of a kind, and you don't find rare breeds under every bush. Whenever I get antsy, Lord, remind me just how worth the wait this special someone will be. In the meantime, give me a double dose of patience!

A PERFECT WORK

But let patience have her perfect work,
that ye may be perfect and entire,
wanting nothing.

JAMES 1:4 KJV

What an amazing verse: "Let patience [perseverance] have her perfect work." Now those are baffling words at first sight. Upon reading them again in a few different translations, the meaning becomes clear: When I endure difficulties yet continue to persevere in the faith, my perseverance pays off in the form of godly character. The same could be said of human endeavors like goals and dreams—the diligent tortoise crosses the finish line while the dawdling hare misses the mark.

Lord, give me the perseverance needed to weather the storms I will surely face in this life. I ask for Your strength to hang in there when the going gets rough.

MORE THAN A SIGN

*May the God of hope fill you with
all joy and peace as you trust in him,
so that you may overflow with hope
by the power of the Holy Spirit.*

ROMANS 15:13

The peace sign has made a fashion comeback, and it's cool to wear it on clothes, a backpack, or whatever. I know that most kids think "world peace" when they see the sign, or just a generic "peace" that means everything and nothing.

The peace You give passes all understanding, Lord. At least that's what You promise in Your Word.

When I'm feeling stressed out or worried about something, wash me in Your peace—the only kind that's really worth anything.

PEACE AND QUIET

"I will give you the treasures of darkness,
riches stored in secret places,
so that you may know that I am the LORD,
the God of Israel, who summons you by name."

ISAIAH 45:3

We live in a noisy world, Lord. From the buzzing of the alarm clock to the chatter of the TV at night, my day is filled with noise clutter. All this excess sound makes me appreciate those few quiet moments that occasionally slip into my life.

Peace and quiet are not qualities most people associate with teens, but I think I need more of them in my life, Lord. Help me to slow down and take time for stillness today, for it's when I'm quiet that I grow most aware of You.

LIKE A RIVER

"If only you had paid attention to my commands,
your peace would have been like a river,
your righteousness like the waves of the sea."

ISAIAH 48:18

I found the phrase "peace like a river" in the Bible and thought about why You chose that particular description, Lord. I think what You're trying to convey is that the peace You give—which Jesus said is "not as the world gives"—flows continuously in the human heart like a river. At least, it *can* flow—as long as we let it.

This is a troubled world we live in, Lord, and people talk about the need for peace. Do they ever stop and think that You can't fabricate peace in dark, turbulent hearts?

Only as we come to know You, individually, do we experience firsthand what it is to feel peace like a river. Father, let that river flow deep within me.

PEACE IN THE HOUSE

If it is possible, as far as it depends on you,
live at peace with everyone.

ROMANS 12:18

Families are hotbeds of strife. Who can't relate to loud arguments that flare over silly things like smelly socks on the bathroom floor or hair left in the shower drain?

I'm a guilty party in these family fights more often than I should be, Lord, and I'm ashamed to admit it. You desire that we live in peace, not just with our family members, but also with the people who populate our larger lives at school and at work.

Today, Lord, I pray for peace in the house. Cause me to be a peacemaker and a peace-keeper every day of my life.

STAYING PURE

Therefore, I urge you, brothers,
in view of God's mercy,
to offer your bodies as living sacrifices,
holy and pleasing to God—
this is your spiritual act of worship.

ROMANS 12:1

The message sent out by the world is loud and clear, "Have sex whenever you want to. Experimentation is good." But I see a different standard in Your Word, Lord. You encourage me to save my sexuality for marriage—for that one special man I may marry someday.

Sometimes I struggle with impure thoughts or want to do things "they" say is okay. But Your Holy Spirit raises a little red flag in my conscience, making the right choice crystal clear. Help me to obey that "still, small voice" inside me and bring honor to You with my thoughts and actions.

I really do want to follow Your rules, Lord. Give me the strength to go against the crowd and take a stand for purity.

ONE OF THE HERD?

*"But small is the gate and
narrow the road that leads to life,
and only a few find it."*

MATTHEW 7:14

It's easy to take a stand from a safe distance or to vow during youth group prayer time that I will not run with the crowd, but the reality of doing that—in the real world—can be much trickier. I need Your strength to stay on the "straight and narrow," Lord. I've heard the still, small voice of the Spirit telling me what's right and what's wrong. Help me to follow through on choices I know are best for me.

Help me to refuse that invitation to the unchaperoned party. Prompt me to "just say no" when someone offers me a free high. Give me the courage not to laugh at dirty jokes at the lunchroom table.

The price of being different can be costly—ask any teenager who refuses to go with the flow. But I'm learning how much more wonderful life is when I follow Your lead rather than the herd going down the wrong road.

MATURITY

There is a way that seems right to a man,
but in the end it leads to death.

PROVERBS 14:12

Not caving in to peer pressure all boils down to maturity, I think, Lord. If I feel secure in who I am—my values and beliefs—then what other people say or do won't matter.

A book I read the other day said maturity is being able to control my emotions when I don't get what I want. That started me thinking, Lord. *How do I react when I don't get my way? How do I behave when someone says bad things about me? Do I stand up to my friends when they are putting someone down?*

Peer pressure may be shouting for me to do one thing, but Your Word offers a clear guideline for right behavior, Lord. Help me to be mature—confident and secure in who I am in You.

CLOTHING CLUES

She is clothed with strength and dignity;
she can laugh at the days to come.
She speaks with wisdom,
and faithful instruction is on her tongue.

PROVERBS 31:25–26

Lord, if I take my cues on how to dress only from popular culture, I may wind up sacrificing modesty for fashion trends. Over and over I hear Christian guys say to girls, "Be careful how you dress—it has a huge effect on us!"

Maybe sometimes we girls are a little ignorant of just how great that effect is—or, worse, we use it to our advantage and try to lure guys through their eyes. Other girls may dress provocatively or bare too much skin, but I know I have a different code to live by, Lord.

At the same time I don't want to be frumpy, so help me to combine my fashion sense with the sensitivity of the Holy Spirit for a style that's both "clean" and cute.

PRAYER POWER

In the morning, O LORD,
you hear my voice;
in the morning I lay my requests before you
and wait in expectation.

PSALM 5:3

Prayer doesn't get a lot of media attention these days, and if you happen to mention it in a crowded hallway at school, you get funny stares. Yet it seems like the greatest firepower a believer has, Lord.

It's comforting to know that I can talk to You no matter where I am—at home in my bedroom or on a noisy school bus. I'm starting to think of prayer as a kind of running dialogue with You. Maybe that's what the apostle Paul meant when he said to "pray without ceasing." What an awesome privilege!

LOOKING OUTWARD

Be careful for nothing;
but in every thing by prayer
and supplication with thanksgiving
let your requests be made known unto God.

PHILIPPIANS 4:6 KJV

So easily I fall into the habit of praying only for myself, Lord, but there's a world of need just in my small circle of friends and family. This one needs a new job; this one's marriage is in trouble. This person is battling cancer and another needs You in their life.

When I was little, I learned rote prayers that I would say every night before falling asleep; they were mechanical but heartfelt. As I've grown, my prayers have grown with me— more conversational, like I'm talking to a friend (I am!). Now I want to stretch my prayer life again to get the focus off myself.

An amazing thing happens whenever I focus on others: Somehow my own needs are always met!

MISSION MINDED

*"Therefore go and make disciples of all nations,
baptizing them in the name of the Father
and of the Son and of the Holy Spirit,
and teaching them to obey everything
I have commanded you."*

MATTHEW 28:19–20

From time to time, we get a missionary zeal at youth group and pray for unreached people groups around the world. It's difficult to stay focused for very long on distant places and people we've never even heard of, but I'm trying to see them as You do, Father.

To You, it's not just a numbers game—X number of new believers worldwide within Y number of years. Rather, I think You're all about the individuals. When I look at a map and locate a remote tribe, I see a name on a continent; You see men, women, and children who don't know You, yet perhaps sense there's something out there greater than themselves.

Today I pray for those people—with real names and personalities—around the world who need You in their lives.

PRAYER CHANGES THINGS—OR CHANGES ME

*"But when you pray, go into your room,
close the door and pray to your Father,
who is unseen. Then your Father, who sees
what is done in secret, will reward you."*

MATTHEW 6:6

Lord, for years I've heard the little saying, "Prayer changes things." But I've also heard people say that prayer doesn't necessarily change *things,* it changes *me.* I'd like to think they're both right, Father.

Thank You for the opportunity You've given me to pray. From my most secret place I can cry out to You whenever I'm hurting. . .I can sing Your praises whenever I'm happy. . . I can request Your help for myself, my family, my friends, and my world.

Whether the prayers actually change the circumstances I face, or whether they cause me to make changes to the world around me, they are accomplishing what You want to see accomplished. And that's reward enough for me, Lord!

DATA INPUT

For as [a person] *thinketh in his heart,
so is he.*

PROVERBS 23:7 KJV

My computer is reliable when it comes to information. Whatever I put into it gets spit back out on demand. I think my brain works much the same way: Data in, data out. Garbage in, garbage out. Good stuff in, good stuff out. Really, this computer analogy applies to my whole life, Lord. Whatever I take in through my five senses and process in my "computer" shapes me as a person.

Do my parents approve of everything I take in? Do You approve? Do I even approve? There's a lot of garbage in the world, and if I'm not careful, I'll easily get desensitized to the bad stuff.

Lord, I want to stay pure in an impure world, and it all starts with my thoughts. Help me to keep a clean slate!

BATHROOM HUMOR

Do not let any unwholesome talk
come out of your mouths,
but only what is helpful for building
others up according to their needs,
that it may benefit those who listen.

EPHESIANS 4:29

I've discovered that living a pure life means more than just avoiding sex. As a Christian teen who wants to honor You, Lord, I also need purity in my thought life, my speech, and in the way I dress.

Teens seem to flock to crude jokes like pigeons to peanuts. Being a part of the group, it's tempting to laugh when everyone else laughs, even though I know I shouldn't. The same goes for everyday speech. Where do I draw the line between okay and not so acceptable?

Lord, put a guard at my lips today, as the Scripture says. Give me the courage to be different, to go against the flow when all the other kids laugh at crude jokes or make suggestive remarks. Being a godly girl means standing apart from the crowd when the crowd opposes You.

TAINTED LOVE

Flee from sexual immorality.
All other sins a man commits
are outside his body,
but he who sins sexually
sins against his own body.

1 CORINTHIANS 6:18

Love that's pure has a right feeling to it. It's not hampered by sinful thoughts or immorality. That's the kind of love I see expressed between couples who honor You, Lord, and it's the kind of love I'm willing to wait for.

I think many Christian teens fall into the trap of thinking they can have it both ways—the excitement of sensual love coupled with the "clean slate" feeling that comes from repentance.

I know Your grace is far-reaching, Father, and nothing I can do will separate me from it. At the same time, Paul said, "Shall we continue in sin, that grace may abound? God forbid." That's pretty strong language. In modern terms, he's saying, "No way! Don't even go there!"

A PURE HEART

Who may ascend the hill of the LORD?
Who may stand in his holy place?
He who has clean hands and a pure heart.

PSALM 24:3–4

Your Word says that You desire "clean hands and a pure heart," Lord. To me, that means hands that neither commit evil nor plot against others and a heart that seeks to do what is right.

I may never have committed a crime, but are my hands always "clean"? Is my heart in the right place with regard to You and other people? There is so much more to purity than just abstaining from sexual sin. With Your help, Lord, let me lead a pure life through-out—in my thoughts and in my actions.

WALKING ON WATER

Then Peter got down out of the boat,
walked on the water and came toward Jesus.
But when he saw the wind,
he was afraid and, beginning to sink,
cried out, "Lord, save me!"
Immediately Jesus reached out his hand
and caught him.
"You of little faith," he said, "why did you doubt?"

MATTHEW 14:29–31

Peter was one brave dude. When I think about how much guts it took to step out of a boat onto water, it amazes me. I read in Scripture that faith the size of a mustard seed is enough to move mountains, but honestly, Lord, I struggle to rely on You even for little things. How did Peter stretch his faith to such a quantum leap?

Today I want to rely on You for the basic stuff, and it might sound mundane, but it's real, Lord. Help me not to worry about that cute guy in class, give me the words to say when someone asks me about my faith, let me pass my math test, and open my eyes to the needs of others.

FATHER KNOWS BEST

"You are my Father, my God,
the Rock my Savior."

PSALM 89:26

That's the title of an old TV show from the '50s, and even though it sounds hokey, it's a pretty good description of my life with You, Lord. You are my Father, and, yes, I have to admit (sometimes grudgingly) that You know what's best for my life.

Relying on You for food, clothing, and shelter sounds so ordinary—I don't really worry about those things. But move into the realm of relationships, self-image, and life choices, and the intensity factor kicks way up.

Since You know what's best for me, Lord, have Your way with my life. My prayer today is for the faith to trust You to work out all the details—big or small.

BIG GIRL NOW

When I was a child, I talked like a child,
I thought like a child, I reasoned like a child.
When I became a man, I put childish ways
behind me. Now we see but a poor reflection
as in a mirror; then we shall see face to face.
Now I know in part; then I shall know fully,
even as I am fully known.

1 CORINTHIANS 13:11–12

We never outgrow our need for You, do we, Father? When I was small, I wanted so much to be grown up, even though I was still just Mom and Dad's little girl. Then I became a "big girl" and thought I didn't need my parents so much anymore. Was I ever wrong!

Just as I've learned how much I still depend on my earthly parents, I'm realizing how much I depend on You, Lord. In fact, the older I get the *more* I seem to need You. Maybe that's because life gets harder with every passing year, even as it brings new joys and accomplishments my way.

Even though I'm a big girl now, help me to rely on You as a little girl relies on her daddy for every need.

SITTING AT YOUR FEET

"Martha, Martha," the Lord answered,
"you are worried and upset about many things,
but only one thing is needed.
Mary has chosen what is better,
and it will not be taken away from her."

LUKE 10:41–42

The story of Martha and Mary has always in-trigued me, Lord. They were both devoted fol-lowers of You, yet displayed different degrees of godly passion for You.

When the group of disciples arrived in Bethany, Martha hurried to prepare food for the hungry travelers and thought her labor was a gift to You. Meanwhile, her sister Mary lazed at Your feet while You talked about the kingdom of God.

The irony to me is that You gently chastised Martha, saying that Mary had chosen what was better. I think You were saying that we have to rely on You for everything—and we learn to rely on You while sitting at Your feet.

Today, Lord, I commit to sit quietly at Your feet for a while and learn from You.

SCHOOL DAZE

*"The waves of death swirled about me;
the torrents of destruction overwhelmed me."*

2 SAMUEL 22:5

Lord, someday I may look back at my school days and laugh, but right now they can be pretty consuming. It's funny how such a small part of life—just four or five years—can wreak either havoc or blessing, depending on what happens within those "hallowed" hallways. I'm consumed with questions like, *Will I be branded a geek? Will I make friends at my new school? Will I get all the electives I planned for? What happens if the other kids don't like me?*

School stress can be a load, Lord, and that's why I need Your help today. Most of all, I pray for the wisdom to keep things in perspective and trust You for the outcome.

Worker Bee

But those who hope in the LORD
will renew their strength.
They will soar on wings like eagles;
they will run and not grow weary,
they will walk and not be faint.

Isaiah 40:31

Twelve years, and then college? Sometimes when I think about how long I've been in school (and how much I have left to go), it wearies me, Lord.

Maybe school is not as intense as it was in the old days, but it's still hard, and I feel like I'm becoming a worker bee. Eight hours of schoolwork, only to come home and work some more. I'm losing myself in all this studying!

When I start to feel overwhelmed with the workload or the subjects themselves, I will call You to the rescue, Lord. Maybe You could send a helper—a tutor or understanding family member—to make sense of the madness, and help get me back on track.

DIFFICULT TEACHERS

*Do not rebuke an older man harshly,
but exhort him as if he were your father.
Treat. . .older women as mothers.*

1 TIMOTHY 5:1–2

No one ever promised that school would be easy, but it was higher math I expected to struggle with, not a teacher! Most of them are great, Lord, but there's that one teacher—You know the one I'm talking about. As I head toward that class every day, I want to duck into the bathroom and never come out. I need Your help!

When my attitude gets out of whack, remind me that You love me even when I'm unlovable and You want me to share that love with others. When I'm tempted to scowl in class, extend to me Your grace, and in turn, help me to extend that grace to my teacher.

MAKING THE GRADE

*But everything should be done
in a fitting and orderly way.*

1 CORINTHIANS 14:40

I just got my report card, Lord, and breathed a sigh of relief! It could have been worse, but I suppose it could have been better, too. Yes, I made decent grades, but when I remember all my activities during this last semester, I know I didn't give school my best effort.

I'll admit that sometimes school falls to last place on my list of priorities. It's always there on a back burner of my mind, but things like relationships and thoughts about how to get that cool summer job easily edge it out. Maybe if I studied harder, I could turn those okay grades into fantastic ones.

Every kid moans and groans about school, but at the same time I know these are years I'll look back on fondly when I'm older. Help me to make the most of them, Lord— grades and all.

REAL BEAUTY

*Your beauty should not come
from outward adornment. . . .
Instead, it should be that of your inner self,
the unfading beauty of a gentle and quiet spirit,
which is of great worth in God's sight.*

1 PETER 3:3–4

Everywhere I go, Lord, I am bombarded with images of what popular culture calls "beautiful." But You remind me in Your word that real beauty starts on the inside—a light that shines outward, a kind and loving spirit.

Whenever I start to compare myself to others, or regard the mirror as my enemy, help me remember that what You think about me matters so much more than the opinions of others. When I put my focus on You, instead of superficial things, I forget to worry about flawless skin or how fashionable my jeans are.

Today, Lord, help me to see myself as You do—someone who is "wonderfully made" and formed in the image of God. What an awesome thought!

LOVING MYSELF

We love because he first loved us.

1 JOHN 4:19

I've heard it said that I have to love myself before I'm capable of loving others fully. But Lord, if I'm honest, I admit that sometimes I don't even like myself—much less love the person called "me."

It's tempting to base my self-worth on what I look like, the girl I see when I look in the mirror. But You remind me that I am so much more than my physical appearance, Lord. Deep down I know that I am worthy of loving and being loved, not because of what I look like but because of who I am—especially who I am in You.

As I go about my day, Lord, help me to love and accept myself just the way I am.

HAIR HANG-UPS

Does not the very nature of things
teach you that if a man has long hair,
it is a disgrace to him,
but that if a woman has long hair, it is her glory?
For long hair is given to her as a covering.

1 CORINTHIANS 11:14–15

It sounds like such a trivial thing, but sometimes my hair gets me depressed, Lord. Sometimes I love it and other times I hate it. What's up with that? It seems silly to get bent out of shape over something like *hair*, but tell that to the zillions of teenage girls who crowd into the bathroom between classes at school.

The other day I came across a Scripture that said a girl shouldn't overfocus on hair when it comes to beauty. At the same time, Your Word calls a woman's hair her "glory," so that can't be a bad thing.

Help me to find a balance between obsessing over my hair and appreciating it for the "natural beauty enhancer" You meant it to be. I know that the real me—the person I am inside—is what really matters.

MEDIA MADNESS

*Charm is deceptive, and beauty is fleeting;
but a woman who fears the LORD
is to be praised.*

PROVERBS 31:30

Lord, sometimes I forget that the current definition of beauty—waiflike bodies and long straight hair—is just a reflection of what our culture and the media call "beautiful." I read somewhere that a long time ago full, rounded bodies were the standard of feminine beauty! All this tells me is that "beauty" can be as subjective as fashion fads that come and go—in one year and out the next. Who wants that type of pressure about their self-image?

Help me to remember that Your Word—not the media—defines what is and is not beautiful. I want to focus on things that really matter: a kind heart, a good attitude, a cheerful personality. A smile that springs from inside and eyes full of the light of the Spirit will never go out of style.

STAYING PURE

It is God's will that you should be sanctified:
that you should avoid sexual immorality;
that each of you should learn to control
his own body in a way that is holy and honorable,
not in passionate lust like the heathen,
who do not know God.

1 THESSALONIANS 4:3–5

There's a saying that if you stick your hand in the cookie jar, you'll eventually end up taking the cookie. For me, that means if I want to avoid premarital sex, I need to avoid situations where I'm more likely to give into pressure from boys or the mentality that says virgins are geeks.

I know You made me for one special man, Lord, and I want to save myself for him. The gift of myself—body and soul—is not something to be given away lightly. Keep me focused on Your standards as I face each day and the temptations it brings.

DATING DILEMMA

Since the day we heard about you,
we have not stopped praying for you
and asking God to fill you with
the knowledge of his will through
all spiritual wisdom and understanding.

COLOSSIANS 1:9

Lord, I know that some girls who have committed themselves to sexual purity have learned the hard way that sex without a lifelong commitment is empty.

Does dating imply a serious enough commitment to engage in a sexual relationship? I guess the answer goes without saying—no! Yet this remains the biggest struggle for Christian teens, and I know I'm just deceiving myself if I think I won't struggle with the sex issue, too.

Lord, help me to listen to the wisdom of my parents and Your Word when it comes to sex. I want to live a life with no regrets over this special gift You have given to husbands and wives—not boyfriends and girlfriends.

SELF-CONTROL

Put to death, therefore,
whatever belongs to your earthly nature:
sexual immorality, impurity, lust,
evil desires and greed, which is idolatry.

COLOSSIANS 3:5

If ever I've needed self-control, Lord, it's now—in these crazy years when my hormones are doing back flips and all the messages around me cry, "Just do it!" I know many girls my age mistake sex for love and throw themselves headlong into foolish relationships. The regrets come later.

Today my prayer is not only for the self-control to say no to temptation but also the desire to say yes to Your concept of true love—the kind that waits until marriage for sex.

Help me to do more than give lip service to Your precepts, Father. I want to live them every day of my life.

A CHANGING FORM

The body is not meant for sexual immorality,
but for the Lord,
and the Lord for the body.

1 CORINTHIANS 6:13

As my body changes, I have to keep adjusting to a new version of "me", Lord. Suddenly I look in the mirror and see not a girl anymore but a young woman. And with each change and just about every passing day, I become more aware of my own sexuality.

I know from the blatant media messages that women can use sex as a tool. They can wield their charm and sensuality like a weapon, making men vulnerable to their wiles. I don't want to be that kind of woman, Father. Instead, help me to keep my sensual self intact until marriage, when the right man will gain the privilege of unlocking my secret self.

Yes, sexuality is powerful, but You intended it to be a thing of beauty and intimacy.

ME, AN EVANGELIST?

Therefore, since we have such a hope,
we are very bold.

2 CORINTHIANS 3:12

Lord, sometimes I get suddenly shy when I know I'm supposed to speak up—about You, that is. Why do I get so tongue-tied when my words might make a difference in someone's life?

I've heard that someone famous once said, "Preach at all times; if necessary use words." Now that sounds more like my style of witnessing, Lord. I want to show people by my life that You are alive and well on Planet Earth.

Help me to live in such a way that people don't just notice the difference in me—they stop and ask about it.

BOLD BELIEVER

In him and through faith in him
we may approach God with
freedom and confidence.

EPHESIANS 3:12

My youth pastor at church encourages us to share our faith. "Be bold!" he exhorts, and I leave youth meetings with enough zeal to last a lifetime. But Lord, You know how quickly I settle back into my familiar routine at home and school, retreating into my Christian shell.

Lord, I've realized that in-your-face evangelism is not my style, nor is it an effective approach with most people. The few times I've shared my faith, it's been a natural outgrowth of conversation with a friend or acquaintance.

For today, Lord, encourage me to follow Jesus' example by being real with people. After all, that's what I'd want someone to be with me.

FOUR SPIRITUAL LAWS?

What good is it, my brothers,
if a man claims to have faith but has no deeds?
Can such faith save him?
But someone will say, "You have faith;
I have deeds."
Show me your faith without deeds,
and I will show you my faith by what I do.

JAMES 2:14, 18

I once heard a talk on the "Four Spiritual Laws" and how they comprise the best approach for witnessing to a stranger about You, Jesus. The thing is, most kids my age can't relate to stuff like this. What we crave more than anything else is reality, and the reality of a changed life—now that's powerful!

As I go about my day, Lord, give me opportunities to talk about my faith in You, but let my actions do most of the talking. More than anything else, I want my life to be "real" for You. If other kids my age see that and realize there's something different about me, maybe they'll want what I've got. You and I know there's plenty to go around!

A Time to Speak

. . .a time to be silent and a time to speak.

Ecclesiastes 3:7

I've always loved the passage in Ecclesiastes that says there's a time for everything under heaven, "a time to be silent and a time to speak." That's wisdom for me right now, Lord, and it comes just when I need it.

Recently I've found myself in situations where I thought I should talk about You, Jesus, but the timing seemed off. For some reason the person wasn't receptive, but I tried to force the gospel anyway. Not surprisingly, it was a botched attempt.

In contrast, I remember other times when I kept silent and just loved the person through my spirit and actions. Later, when their own spirit was ready, conversation about You flowed easily.

Help me to always be sensitive to the Holy Spirit when sharing my faith.

FORBIDDEN FRUIT

*But the fruit of the Spirit is
love, joy, peace, patience, kindness, goodness,
faithfulness, gentleness and self–control.*

GALATIANS 5:22–23

Why is it that the thing that is most forbidden is so alluring to me? Am I the only one out there who struggles with sin, Lord? I know our culture has almost done away with the word *sin*, but I also know it's alive and well everywhere I look—and I don't have to look too far from my own life.

As I go about my day, Lord, keep me from sinning against You. The psalmist had a cool idea: "I have hidden your word in my heart that I might not sin against You." That's my goal and my prayer today, Father.

WARNING OTHERS

Blow the trumpet in Zion;
sound the alarm on my holy hill.
Let all who live in the land tremble,
for the day of the LORD is coming.
It is close at hand.

JOEL 2:1

I came across this verse in the Old Testament that says to "sound the alarm" when danger is approaching. If the watchman didn't do his job, the people killed on his watch would be his responsibility. That's a heavy-duty thought, Lord, but it started me thinking, *Do I sometimes watch a friend walk right into danger— something sinful—and not warn her? What is my responsibility to sound the alarm?*

Lord, teach me how to speak up when I see a friend skating on thin ice, whether it's her choice of boyfriend, a fascination with the supernatural, or a try-and-see attitude toward drugs. Being the whistle-blower may not make me popular, but it could help a friend make the right choice.

The Best Antidote

But my eyes are fixed on you,
O Sovereign LORD; in you I take refuge.

PSALM 141:8

I've learned that the best antidote to sinning is to keep my eyes focused on You, Lord. If You are constantly in my thoughts, how will I fall into error or do something shameful—something I know will grieve Your Holy Spirit within me?

The good news is that I don't have to "grin and bear it" whenever temptation comes my way. Yes, there will be times when resisting temptation will take Your strength—not mine—but if I keep You ever before me, as the psalmist said, sin won't even look attractive to me.

Make my appetite for sin diminish, Father, even as You increase my desire for godly things. I want to be a vessel of honor and purity all the days of my life.

WRITING IN THE SAND

*But Jesus bent down and started to write
on the ground with his finger.
When they kept on questioning him,
he straightened up and said to them,
"If any one of you is without sin,
let him be the first to throw a stone at her."*

JOHN 8:6–7

Jesus, Your behavior often baffled the people of Your day, especially the religious bigwigs. I love reading the story of the woman caught in adultery and how You responded when the Pharisees brought her to You for punishment. You knelt down and started writing in the sand.

I wonder what You wrote? Did You leave some sort of message there in the sand—a message that would prick the people's consciences and soften their hearts? Or were You merely showing the Pharisees that You had no intention of throwing a stone at the woman and that neither should they?

Lord, You are so loving and gracious that it overwhelms me at times. No, I've never committed adultery, but You've seen the other sins in my life—and forgiven them, every one.

BEING MY BEST

*Whatever your hand finds to do,
do it with all your might.*

ECCLESIASTES 9:10

You've given me so many gifts, Lord, that
sometimes I take them for granted. Whenever
I'm tempted to slack off at school or give a
halfhearted effort in my talent, remind me to
raise the bar a little higher. I need these occasional adjustments in both my attitude and my
performance.

Actually, I've begun to see my time and
talents as tools for honoring You. Doing less
than my best is not worth it in the long run.
I'm so glad Your Word reminds me to work
diligently, regardless of the task. When I do, I
feel Your pleasure.

With such a high standard in mind, I'd be
crazy to offer You less than my best!

DISTINCT GIFTS

*For God's gifts and his call
are irrevocable.*

ROMANS 11:29

What an awesome feeling it is to find something I'm good at, Lord! For years I struggled
to be someone I'm not. I watched other girls
who were good at something and thought, *I
want to do that, too!* But then I discovered that
I had no knack for it at all. The realization
sent me into a downward spiral, until I found
my own special talent.

My new revelation is that You've implanted
gifts within each of us, Lord, and they can't
all be the same thing. I'm figuring out what it
is I excel at, and it encourages me to know my
gifts are just as meaningful as someone else's.
I don't ever want to be boastful or arrogant
about the things I do well; I simply want to
bless You and others through my talents. Let
me use them for Your glory, Lord.

HONING MY SKILLS

As iron sharpens iron,
so one man sharpens another.

PROVERBS 27:17

The verse that says "iron sharpens iron" used to fly right over my head, but now I'm starting to understand what it means, Lord— when I'm around people who challenge me to be my best, I become my best.

Whatever skills and talents I possess, I want to hone them to use for Your glory, Lord. It's awesome to think that I may be sharpening the edges of a friend at the same time she's sharpening me. Thanks for giving me friends and mentors who can help me to be my best.

WORK OF ART

For we are God's workmanship,
created in Christ Jesus to do good works,
which God prepared in advance for us to do.

EPHESIANS 2:10

Ecclesiastes says, "Whatever your hand finds to do, do it with all your might." I've made a wonderful discovery, Lord. The things You've gifted me to do well, I love to do anyway—and always want to do "with all my might." What a kind and generous Father You are! It blows me away to think that I am innately gifted to do good works that You've prepared for me to do.

Fueled by this motivation, it's easy to perform my best because I know that I have become a living work of art. Never let me get boastful about my talents or abilities, Lord. Instead, lovingly remind me that every good gift comes from above.

When I look around me and see the varied gifts and talents my friends possess, I rejoice all over again. We are rich beyond belief!

PRIORITIES

Be very careful, then, how you live. . .
making the most of every opportunity,
because the days are evil.

EPHESIANS 5:15–16

Making the most of my time is not something I've ever worried too much about. But with school, homework, family, church, friends, and time with You, Lord, I'm starting to see where the term "time management" came from. Do other girls my age have so many things to juggle in life, too?

Lord, help me to prioritize my time so that the things that matter most won't get my leftover energy. I've only got one life to live, and I want to live it well!

FAMILY HOURS

Therefore, as God's chosen people,
holy and dearly loved,
clothe yourselves with compassion,
kindness, humility, gentleness and patience.

COLOSSIANS 3:12

Lord, if there's one area of my life that gets my leftovers, it's my family. I'm ashamed to admit this, but it's true (and You know it already). These are the people I share a home with, the ones I sit across from at dinner, yet they know me less than my best friends do. In the past few years I've grown distant from my family. I guess part of that is the independence we establish as teenagers—sort of like weaning ourselves from the nest.

But I think I've taken it a little too far. My family and I pass each other in the hall like virtual strangers, each retreating to our own bedrooms to talk on the phone or dial up on the Internet.

Starting today, Lord, I want to get reacquainted with the members of my family. They are, after all, my own flesh and blood, and I love them.

FLYING TIME

There is a time for everything,
and a season for every activity under heaven.

ECCLESIASTES 3:1

The phrase "Time flies" used to make me wrinkle my brow in puzzlement. When I was a little kid, time seemed to drag, but now I'm starting to understand that time really does fly, Lord.

Already, I look back on the past year of my life and wonder where the time has flown to. I gaze at my geeky picture in last year's yearbook and think, *What happened to that girl?*

Time is precious, Lord. Help me to make the most of the days You've allotted to my life.

TITHING TIME

*"Bring the best of the firstfruits of your soil
to the house of the LORD your God."*

EXODUS 23:19

Someone told me about the concept of tithing
my time—meaning that I give You ten percent
of my time, and ideally the "firstfruits" of my
day. What will happen if I start each day with
You, Lord? Friends who have tried this come
back enthusiastic about the results—somehow,
if they are faithful to start the day with You,
there's always time to fit everything else into
the hours remaining.

I've heard the same is true with tithing
income—if I'm faithful to give You a tenth of
what I earn, You will not only provide all my
needs but also open the "windows" of heaven
and pour out blessing on my life. Does the
same principle apply to tithing time? I want
to find out!

Lord, today I will commit myself to spending time with You before the rest of the day
gets cluttered with activities. Thank You for *always* being ready and willing to meet with me!

BELIEVING GOD

Hear my cry, O God;
listen to my prayer.

PSALM 61:1

I find a strange tug-of-war raging inside me,
Lord. I want to believe Your Word—all Your
promises—but I have a hard time trusting You.
You, the Creator of the universe, the God of all
creation! Yet somehow I worry that You'll be
too busy to bother with my measly little world
or some silly request I throw up to heaven.

I think trust is like a muscle. The more
you use it, the stronger it grows. Little by little,
grow my trust in You until I have no room
for doubt left in my heart. I want to be so
wrapped in Your presence, Lord, that my faith
never wavers again.

REBOUNDING

Trust in him at all times, O people;
pour out your hearts to him,
for God is our refuge.

PSALM 62:8

When guys or girls immediately start dating a new person after getting their hearts broken by someone else, we call it rebounding. It's usually a halfhearted effort that results in a shallow relationship.

Sometimes I think my trust in You follows a similar pattern, Lord. I get my hopes up about something only to be disappointed in the end. I blame You for letting me down, sulk and pout, then rebound into a new level of trust. But here's the difference: Instead of growing shallow, my relationship with You actually gets stronger as I realize You are growing me up.

No, I can't get everything I want in life, but I'm realizing I get everything I need from You—and some cool surprises along the way!

CHAIR POWER

*But I trust in your unfailing love;
my heart rejoices in your salvation.*

PSALM 13:5

I've heard the example given that whenever we sit in a chair, we "trust" that the chair will hold us up. Why? Because it has never let us down before, and because it was built to hold human weight. The chair's four legs give it stability and strength, but take away one of those legs and we would go crashing to the floor!

In the same way, help me to trust You, Lord, simply and completely. Let me trust You, because You've never let me down before and because You are "built" to hold me up when I stumble and fall.

Thank You for Your trustworthiness, Father. Not many things in this world are dependable anymore, but You never fail to provide, to bless, to protect, to encourage, and to love.

TRUST AND OBEY

This is love for God:
to obey his commands.
And his commands are not burdensome.

1 JOHN 5:3

It's funny how often those two things—trust and obedience—go together in the Bible. You don't simply call us to a life of trust, Lord; You call us to a life of trust *and* obedience.

People talk about "greasy grace"—having the license to sin because we know You'll forgive us later. But Paul reacted strongly when he heard the believers of Rome discuss this very issue. What they didn't understand—and what I'm just beginning to understand—is that we obey You because we love You, not because You are a harsh taskmaster. We trust You because You are trustworthy, but unless we couple that faith with obedience to Your will, we make a lie of the Truth.

Lord, help me to be quick to obey and eager to trust You in every facet of my life.

Out of the Pit

Out of the depths I cry to you, O LORD.

PSALM 130:1

I'm hurting inside, Lord, and it feels like I'm deep in a pit with no way out. The sky seems darker, and I move in slow motion all day long. When will the pain go away?

If I'm honest with myself, I know that this episode of sadness will pass, too. Things may not be perfect tomorrow, but You are still my God and You give my life purpose. Whenever I'm down, remind me that You're working behind the scenes to work "together for good to them that love God, to them who are the called according to His purpose."

SHARING THE PAIN

He was despised and rejected by men,
a man of sorrows,
and familiar with suffering.
Like one from whom
men hide their faces he was despised,
and we esteemed him not.

ISAIAH 53:3

Sometimes I hurt so badly, Jesus, that I can't even cry out. You know what it's like to hurt, too, Lord. I've read that You were a man of sorrows, one well acquainted with grief. Yet You comforted others more than anything else while You walked on this earth. How can I become a comforter when I myself need comforting?

I'm taking clues from Your life as much as I can, Lord. As I spend time with You, pour into my life the love and grace that will help heal someone else when the occasion arises. Let me be a light giver even when I've spent time in the darkness.

GROWING STRONG

Consider it pure joy, my brothers,
whenever you face trials of many kinds,
because you know that the testing
of your faith develops perseverance.

JAMES 1:2–3

Lord, it's storming outside and the combination of the dark sky, violent wind, and heavy rain seems to depict the turmoil and pain in my heart right now. I feel like one of the young oaks that we planted in our yard as they are whipped relentlessly by the storm's great force. I've seen them survive other storms, and after each one, it seems they are a little bit taller, a little bit thicker, a little bit stronger.

Just as wind and rain toss a young tree about, forcing its roots to go deeper, I'm discovering that hard times in my life make me a stronger person than I was before. When my heart is broken and the pain seems unbearable, Lord, You are able to mold me from the brokenness into someone better—someone who will be able to persevere through life's next storm, relying on You to hold me up.

IS LIFE AGAINST ME?

But who are you, O man,
to talk back to God?
"Shall what is formed say to him who formed it,
'Why did you make me like this?' "

ROMANS 9:20

Most of the time I feel like my life is pretty together. But right now I'm feeling like it is anything but. In fact, I feel like all of life is against me. Whatever expectations I had seem to have fallen flat. Is destiny plotting my failure?

I know this all sounds dramatic, Lord, but I'm really hurting right now. I need a double dose of Your grace and peace. Help me not to question Your goodness in this situation. Help me to trust that even this dark hour is part of Your loving plan for me.

THRILL RIDE

You have made known to me the path of life;
you will fill me with joy in your presence,
with eternal pleasures at your right hand.

PSALM 16:11

My biggest fear is living an "unlived" life. There's a great big world out there, and I want to embrace it with all the gusto I've got! At the same time, the world generally doesn't follow Your commands, Lord. How can I find a balance?

Make my life an adventure, Father, but keep me within the safe boundaries of righteous living. I know a true adventure—like a thrill ride at the fair—has both ups and downs. Help me to embrace both good times and bad. As long as You're with me, I can face anything.

FINDING MY WAY

There is surely a future hope for you,
and your hope will not be cut off.

PROVERBS 23:18

As a teenager, thoughts of a future career are starting to take shape in my mind, Lord. Suddenly that distant grown-up phase of life is not so far off anymore. Soon it'll be my turn to make my way in the world. Will I be ready for it? What will my contribution be?

Lord, help me to find my way through the maze of choices I will face in the next few years. The decisions I make today may have lifelong repercussions, and I want to choose wisely.

INTERACTING WITH
THE WORLD

*Our conscience testifies that we have conducted
ourselves in the world,
and especially in our relations with you,
in the holiness and sincerity that are from God.
We have done so not according to
worldly wisdom but according to God's grace.*

2 CORINTHIANS 1:12

Even though sometimes I think it would be much easier, Lord, I don't want to hide from the world like some Christians think we should. They think we will be tainted by worldly ways if we don't completely separate ourselves, but Your Word tells us that we should be *in* the world—how else can we share You with the people who need You most?—but not *of* it. That's a fine line, but one we will never cross if we keep our focus on You.

Jesus, You did not hide from the world. You came into this world and died to save me, but proved that You are not of it when you rose again. Thank You for giving me that same assurance—that through You I am also in this world but not of it.

A CHANGING PLACE

"For I know the plans I have for you,"
declares the LORD,
"plans to prosper you and not to harm you,
plans to give you hope and a future."

JEREMIAH 29:11

The news on TV scares me, Lord. This world is a frightening place, spinning out of control toward a final countdown. Rampant crime, freak acts of nature, people out of control, nations plotting destruction—it's enough to keep me up at night.

I suppose none of this is new to You, Lord. The world has been an evil place since Adam and Eve sinned. But lately it does seem that things are getting worse faster than they used to. Is the timetable of the world speeding up? Is the clock ticking too swiftly?

Only You know the future, Father, and so I have to trust my life and times to You. You said in Your Word that You so loved the world that You gave Your only Son to redeem it. My prayer for today is that the world will turn to You before it's too late.

SECURITY IN
AN INSECURE WORLD

*Even though I walk
through the valley of the shadow of death,
I will fear no evil, for you are with me;
your rod and your staff, they comfort me.*

PSALM 23:4

I watched a scary movie last night (I know, I know), and now I'm feeling jumpy, Lord. Did my parents lock the doors before going to bed? Is my window secure? Am I safe at all?

From conversations I've had with friends, it seems a lot of kids worry these days. I suppose it's the sign of the times. I live in a dangerous world, and worry comes naturally to me. Yet You tell me not to worry about anything, Lord—not food, clothing, shelter, physical protection, or what to say or do in a crisis—because You will provide for all my needs.

Whenever I get the worry jitters, remind me just how big You are, Lord. Though the world around me may be going nuts, I'm safe in the palm of Your hand.

LET IT GO

Commit your way to the LORD;
trust in him and he will do this:
He will make your
righteousness shine like the dawn,
the justice of your cause like the noonday sun.

PSALM 37:5–6

Lord, I've heard the phrase "Let go and let God." Boy, if only it were that easy. As soon as I start to trust You with something, I want to snatch it back and take care of things myself. The only problem is that I make things worse than before!

I remember a devotional I read once that said if you're going to give something to God, you've got to unclench your fists. That's me, Lord—always holding on tightly.

Help me learn to let go, Father, and turn my worries into a childlike faith in You.

REPEAT PROMISES

"Therefore I tell you, do not worry about
your life, what you will eat or drink;
or about your body, what you will wear.
Is not life more important than food,
and the body more important than clothes?"

MATTHEW 6:25

When I flip through the Scriptures, I see again and again words of promise in the face of human worries. In Your gentle voice, You tell me, "Do not worry. . .don't let your heart be troubled. . .trust in me. . .do not look at the prosperity of the wicked. . .cast all your cares upon me. . .consider it pure joy. . . ."

Could there be any doubt that You are for me in a world so against me? Do I need to worry after these repeated promises? Obviously not, yet my human weakness wants to look down at the water as Peter did, rather than keep my eyes on You and walk steadily on.

Father, thank You that I don't need to worry about anything. You have made that abundantly clear in Your Word. Now just help me to believe it—really and truly—every moment of my life.

DON'T WORRY, BE HAPPY

*Cast all your anxiety on him
because he cares for you.*

1 PETER 5:7

A goofy song from the '80s told us not to worry but to be happy instead. I'm sure the guy didn't intend to be scriptural, but he really was, wasn't he, Lord? Every time Your Word mentions worry, You follow it with an injunction not to indulge in this wasteful activity—then tell us why we can depend on You.

Few things are as automatic as the song implies, but there's a lot of truth in that quirky little tune. You tell me to cast all my care on You, simply because You care for me and want to make my load light. I wonder sometimes how often we actually live the abundant life You talked about, Jesus. Are we close but miss the mark because of our crippling worries?

Today, Father, I ask You to take the truckload of worries from my life and give me Your joy and peace instead. Thank You for wanting to care for me.

Old Testament

NEW TESTAMENT

NOTES

NOTES